Published by:
Breck Press
PO Box 536
Pioneertown, CA 92268

sandirosemiller.com

Library of Congress Cataloging-in-Publication:
2004099588

Sandi Rose Miller—
The Art of Living ~ Feng Shui YOUR Way!

p. cm
ISBN-13: 978-0-9747767-1-2
1. Feng Shui   2. Decoration & Ornament
3. Decorating & Furnishing   I. Title
2024

Copyright 2005 by Sandi Rose Miller
All rights reserved. No part of this book shall be reproduced, stored in a retrieval system, or transmitted by any means, electronic, mechanical, photocopying, recording, or otherwise, without written permission from the publisher.

Printed in the United States of America

1 3 5 7 9 10 8 6 4 2

Cover design: Lisa Wysocky

To contact Sandi regarding speaking engagements, podcast and public appearances:
breckgirl10@gmail.com

*For my loving son,
Wyatt J.R. Miller,
the light of my life.*

*And for my darling grandmother,
Georgia Virginia Herring,
who taught by example the true meaning
of beauty, nobility and grace.*

In Gratitude

My heartfelt thanks for the love, support and input of my family and friends during the years it took to create and grow this book. So many have contributed to the texture, focus and completion of this project and for everything each has contributed, I am deeply grateful.

An enormous debt of gratitude goes to Beth McCarthy, not only for being a brilliant yoga teacher, but also for introducing me to her incredibly creative husband and my editor, Dennis McCarthy. For the many candles burned at both ends helping me edit, create, fine-tune and birth this manuscript, I am grateful beyond words.

To my initial readers whose insightful comments and tactful suggestions helped shape this book, my sincere thanks to Brian Humphrey, Rev. Peggy Price, Jack Barnard, Patricia Helgevold and John Koster. And to my Breck Girl bud, Tiffanie Williams for her final editing touches and for taking over the reins on the cover design with such grace and ease, my heartfelt thanks and much love.

To my original Feng Shui teacher and mentor, Terah Kathryn Collins, much gratitude, respect and admiration for introducing me to a common sense, user-friendly, westernized approach to Feng Shui that has given me a wonderful foundation to build upon.

Contents

Introduction 9

Section One

The Art of Environmental Flow 29
How Do You Want Your Life to Be? 30
Feng Shui = Intention in Physical Form 32
Your Environment Reflects You! 35
Live With What You Love 36
Negative Memories 37
How is Feng Shui Different from Interior Design? 40
The Importance of a Nurturing Atmosphere in Your Environment 41
Does Your Space Fit You? 46
Getting Started with Environmental Feng Shui 48
Environmental Checklist 49
Clutter 53
Incomplete Cycles of Action 56
De-cluttering Techniques 57
Clutter Clearing Tips 61
Specific Applications 64
Entrances 64
The Importance of Color 67
Plants 68
Mirrors 70
Kitchens 73
Bathrooms 75
Bedrooms 76
Bedroom Tips 77
Offices 80
Helpful Office Tips 82
Summary of Environmental Tips 84
Environmental Comfort Survey 86

Section Two

The Art of Mental Flow	89
Creating Mental Flow With Inner Feng Shui	91
Self-nurturing	93
Awareness	95
Change Your Thinking, Change Your Life	98
Helpful Tips for Changing Root Thoughts	103
Your Life is a Mirror	104
Thoughts Made Manifest	106
Fear = Mental Clutter	108
Dreams and Goals: Things to Try	112
Fears and Concerns: Things to Try	114
Acting on Your Intentions	117
Action: Three Things to Try	119
Keeping Promises, Creating Success	120
Response-Ability	123
Judgment: The High Cost of Needing to be Right	129
Non-Judgment: Things to Try	130
The Healing Power of Self Forgiveness	132
Forgiveness: Things to Try	136
The Power of Gratitude	138
Gratitude: Things to Try	142
Creating Lasting Change: Attitude Tips for Tough Times	143
Keeping Momentum: Things to Try	147
Summary of Mental Flow Tips	150
Attitude Survey	154
In Summary	156
Old Chinese Proverb	159

Introduction

For nearly three decades, I worked in the entertainment industry as a television commercial actress, singer, spokesmodel and mistress of ceremonies. In my mid-40's, the universe made it abundantly clear to me that it was time for a career change. I was intuitively guided to the study of Feng Shui. To my surprise, I found I had been instinctively practicing Feng Shui all my life, I just didn't know my preference for how an environment should be arranged, had a name!

After graduating from the prestigious Western School of Feng Shui, my practice as a Feng Shui specialist grew rapidly. I developed a unique style of combining "outer" Feng Shui with "inner" Feng Shui and was consistently rewarded with my clients achieving outstanding results from our consultations. Yet, I had been unable to find any Feng Shui books I could recommend that addressed in depth the essential combination of inner and outer Feng Shui as a technique for attracting abundance as well as personal abundance. It was then that I realized it must be *my* book to write.

> *"Quality of life cannot be achieved by taking the right shortcut, because there is no shortcut! But there is a path..."*
>
> - Stephen R. Covey

The Art of Living is the culmination of many years of personal and professional experience, research and development. These simple, time-tested techniques and tips can help eliminate years of unnecessary misfortune. I've created a formula that really works and the key is: the more you work it, the more it works for you! All you have to do is follow the steps and implement them as precisely and consistently as possible. It's that simple.

You don't even need to believe this information will create positive change in your life for it to do so. Just do your best to be consistent and thorough in your application of the principles and watch your life continue to improve. Remember, the more you work it, **THE MORE IT WORKS!**

To get the most from this material, you will need to become involved with it as deeply as possible. You will need to closely examine your attitudes, beliefs, intentions, motives and habits. Authentic transformation is a highly introspective process. It is impossible to get deeply immersed in profound truths and emerge unchanged. I am absolutely confident this book can help close the gap between how your life is today and how you wish it to be in the future.

The steps contained within are not complicated nor is the information new. What is new, is the particular combination of information, action steps and instructions specifically designed to enhance and radically change the quality of your life. It is the synergy or the relationship between these steps that is the power behind this specific and unique formula. It is the way in which each step serves the other. When you practice these tips and techniques and make them a regular part of your life, when you live it, your life will change for the better. You'll get out what you put in. YOU CAN COUNT ON IT!

Feng Shui: The Ancient Environmental Science of the Future

Once upon a time, not so very long ago, the now widely-popular environmental science called Feng Shui (pronounced "fung shway") was thought to be shrouded in mystery and superstition and mostly practiced by unconventional, metaphysical or "woo woo" types of folks. How times have changed!

Feng Shui has now become as mainstream as interior design in many places. It is now as normal for homeowners to have their home professionally "feng shuied" as it is to have an interior designer assist in curtain fabric and upholstery selection. Feng Shui is fast becoming a household term and its application as routine as any other essential home design/enhancement practice.

Feng Shui literally means "wind and water." It is often described as the ancient art of living in harmony with our natural surroundings. Feng Shui is widely believed to have originated in China, but over the years I have discovered that virtually every culture in the world has their own version of Feng Shui particularly suited to their individual heritage. Often, our first brush with the many different forms of Feng Shui can seem confusing, foreign and even sometimes contradictory. However, it has been my experience that, while the many varying styles of Feng

Shui seem at first glance to be quite different from one another, the underlying principles of all schools of Feng Shui are really quite similar. Karen Kingston, a popular expert in environmental energy, suggests that all versions of Feng Shui give you basically the same result in the end, harmoniously balanced "Chi" or energy.

Feng Shui is based on thousands of years of practical application and observation of the way an individual's environmental energy (ener/Chi) interacts with their personal energy (inner/Chi). I've found Feng Shui to be a reliable tool for manipulating physical surroundings to more accurately suit each person's unique personality for the purpose of attracting abundance on all levels and encouraging fate in the most favorable and harmonious direction. Bottom line, Feng Shui is about creating energetically balanced environments that nourish our souls and support our personal growth, providing us optimum advantage to be all we can *be*, and fostering opportunities to accomplish all we came here to *do*.

"First we shape our houses, then our houses shape us."

- Winston Churchill

If you are familiar with the concepts in Yoga, Tai Chi, Qiqong or other physical balancing practices, then you know their central purpose is to awaken stagnant areas of Chi in your body. Feng Shui applies a very similar concept to the re-arrangement of your home or work environment, or any area where you spend your time. The aim of Feng

Shui is to awaken and energize stagnant areas of Chi, resulting in a more balanced state of being. All of us can make simple, affordable changes in our homes and workplaces that will spark our natural potential to be more alive, receptive and focused. In these rapidly changing and uncertain times, simple Feng Shui adjustments can help create stability, clarity, prosperity, peace and joy.

Yet, Feng Shui isn't magic. It is a tool, that when used properly, brings surprising and positive results that may *seem* like magic as your environment begins to work *for* you rather than against you. It helps create an atmosphere that greets you like a warm embrace each time you enter your cozy, uplifting and nurturing "home for the soul."

How are things going in your life right now? Is your career turning out to be much less financially and personally rewarding than you thought it would be? Are *you* falling short of your expectations? Are things in the relationship department cooling down, getting too complicated or too hot to handle? Is your health less vibrant than you would like? Do you feel drained, exhausted much of the time? According to Feng Shui principles, the arrangement of objects in your environment has a huge impact on many essential aspects of your life and may have a great deal to do with how your life is currently going for you. If your home or work environment is in chaos, brimming with disorganized piles of paper and incomplete projects amidst a sea of haphazardly-placed furniture, chances are your financial, physical, and emotional well-being will be an unfortunate, yet accurate, reflection of this environmental tornado.

Feng Shui is based on the philosophy that everything is composed of energy called Chi. When the Chi in an environment is not flowing and "pooling" properly, it often results in personal dis-harmony, dis-tress and dis-ease. The intention of Feng Shui is to balance environmental Chi by eliminating areas of stuck, stagnant Chi resulting in greater productivity, prosperity, peace of mind, happiness and health for its fortunate occupants. Feng Shui experts use an ancient tool called a Bagua Map that functions as a guide for the enhancement and placement of objects as well as suggesting beneficial colors and shapes based on the Bagua's layout for each individual environment. Every area in the map coincides with a specific life interest such as relationships, wealth, health, creativity and wisdom. The implementation of Chi enhancements such as particular colors, textures, plants, mirrors, lighting and even soothing or uplifting sounds are also used to promote and establish the harmonious flow of environmental Chi in each Bagua area.

The intricacies of applying Feng Shui effectively can take many years to learn. However, learning basic concepts is easily doable and will bring immediate harmony and alignment to your environmental energy as well as your life. It is *not* necessary to understand or even know about a Bagua map, or have decades of experience to start improving your living and working environment to begin reaping the rewards of balanced Chi. Personalized Bagua maps and years of experience can be applied later if you choose a more intensive application.

As a professional Feng Shui consultant for many years, I can attest to the incredibly powerful experience of living and working in an environmentally balanced home and office. However, it seems to me the last thing needed these days is another confusing "How To" book on Feng Shui. That is why you will not find a lot of rigid or specific Feng Shui "do's and don'ts" in these pages. The suggestions offered here have been proven to produce a positive environmental energy shift, when properly implemented, many times instantaneously. They may simply seem like "concentrated common sense" and you may find yourself wondering, "Why didn't I think of that before?" I have done my best to take the guesswork out of the basic Chi enhancement process so you don't need to worry whether or not you are "doing it right." In the pages that follow, I have distilled the most powerful principles of Feng Shui down into a user-friendly form ready for immediate application and benefit.

In the future, should you find yourself drawn to studying the multitude of books, tapes, classes and other sources of information available for you to deepen your understanding and application skills of this ancient art of placement, I would heartily encourage you do so. However, right now the only book you will need to begin enjoying the wonderfully invigorating, nurturing and auspicious benefits of Feng Shui is the *one you hold in your hands*.

What is Chi?

"Being born with good looks is not as important as being born with a good destiny. Being born with a good destiny is not as important as having a kind heart. Having a kind heart is not as important as having a positive state of Chi."

- Ancient Chinese saying

Thousands of years ago in China, people believed that Chi, an invisible energy force, was responsible for the way particular locations thrived more than others, making them more desirable and inhabitable. They thought Chi was the single most important factor influencing their lives for better or worse. In their bodies, they believed that the level of balance and flow of the seven specific concentrations of Chi (called Chakras) would determine their level of good health and good fortune.

One ancient and still popular method of unblocking and balancing the flow of stuck Chi in the body is the expert use of acupuncture needles allowing the body to heal itself more effectively. Practicing traditional physical disciplines such as Tai Chi, Yoga or Qigong that encourage Chi to flow freely and create a sense of well being is another method of balancing Chi. Also, meditation in whatever form you prefer helps establish a healthy flow of Chi, mentally and spiritually. It was discovered that when Chi is balanced and abundant in our bodies and environment, we quite naturally feel happy and content.

Chi is a concept largely unknown in Western culture but one that figures prominently in cultures of the East. Traditionally, it is considered the universal life force or "cosmic breath" (energy, prana, mana, ki, spirit) of all living things: human, animal, vegetable and mineral as well as environmental, ecological and astrological. According to both Ayurvedic and traditional Chinese medicines, good health is dependent on the unimpeded flow of Chi in the energy system of the body. It is considered the silent force permeating all of nature; the magnificent energy flowing through all living things.

> *"The seed of all things lies buried within us until the gift of mana is offered to it."*
>
> - Kristin Zambucka, *Ano Ano, the Seed*

Bottom line: Chi flows through *all* things determining the difference between being alive or being dead. Chi travels through our bodies carrying our thoughts, ideas and emotions similar to the way our blood progresses along smaller and smaller pathways until it influences every cell of our being. People increasingly experience amazing success improving their health through simply changing the way they *think* because our attitudes and beliefs are continually and constantly having a subtle influence on the quality of our cells.

"All of your thoughts, all of your emotions are biochemical realities in your body. Changing your thoughts literally changes your brain chemistry."

- Dr. Christian Northrup

Even though Chi may not always be easy to see, it is quite easy to feel or sense its effects. Your personal Chi (I call inner/Chi) is really nothing more than your own personal energy. Your inner/Chi is easily influenced not only by your thoughts, but also by the Chi of the foods you eat, the Chi of the people you surround yourself with and the Chi of the environments you live and work in. Your inner/Chi gives color to your face, sparkle to your eyes and movement in your limbs. Whether you are consciously aware of it or not, every minute of every day, your environment either uplifts and nurtures your inner/Chi or drains and depletes you. And, even if you are unaware, or become less aware over time of how the ener/Chi (environmental Chi) of a particular space is effecting you, you are not being *less* affected by its energy!

"Where we are is as important as who we are... interaction with the world is impaired when our surroundings are not nourishing."

- Nancylee Wydra, *Feng Shui: The Book of Cures*

As your personal inner/Chi becomes more balanced, your attitudes and thinking patterns improve and your emotions become increasingly stabilized and harmonious. You'll begin noticing more wonderful, exciting opportunities naturally coming your way. New "wins" reinforce your positive feelings and your inner/Chi expands as a beneficial renewal cycle is born. Since your inner/Chi is basically the foundation of your life, enhancing this powerful life force with Feng Shui is essential for maximizing your destiny. The more balanced your environmental (ener/Chi) and personal (inner/Chi), the greater your awareness and clarity around new possibilities and opportunities, as well as the essential focus and wisdom required to take decisive, appropriate and timely action.

> "The building you live in is inanimate in one sense, but every atom within it is pulsating with life. It has its own story in which you and the people you live with are characters, just as the structure is a silent character in your biography. You provide the opportunity for life to continue in this place. It in turn gives you a place to cultivate your soul."
>
> - Victoria Moran, *Shelter for the Spirit*

One way to think of environmental ener/Chi is as if it were a gentle stream of water flowing into a room. If, for example, the main entrance/door to the room is too cramped or cannot open completely, the ener/Chi flow will be reduced to a trickle. If the flow is slow, some energy-starved areas take on a stagnant, uninviting, limiting feeling. If the flow is too fast, as in a long, straight hallway or a front entrance that opens up directly into a view of the back door, shooting ener/Chi like an arrow from one end of the house to the other, you may find you never feel like spending time in that area because the energy is moving too quickly to feel comfortable. The ideal solution or "cure" is to create opportunities for the ener/Chi to meander and "pool" occasionally throughout the space just as naturally as a healthy, babbling brook.

Other factors influencing and altering ener/Chi flow by slowing it down or speeding it up are: the physical shape of an object (sharp or soft, angular or curvaceous); the amount of furniture in a room (too cramped or too Spartan); color (warm or cool tones) or the lack thereof and the amount of light (natural or artificial) that is reflected in the room. Even the fabrics, textures and construction materials used in a space as well as ener/Chi enhancers (water features, sound soothers, mirrors, plants) convey many different levels of ener/Chi.

> "We can orchestrate our fate by manipulating an environment."
>
> - Nancylee Wydra

How Chi Flows

> "Feng Shui is another tool given to us by the universe to help us overcome our difficulties, support our challenges, and smooth over life's conflicts."
>
> - Nancy SantoPietro, *Feng Shui: Harmony by Design*

Essentially, practicing effective Feng Shui is all about arranging our space so that the ener/Chi feels balanced and flows harmoniously, positioning us to take optimal advantage of positive ener/Chi flow.

> "We are not separate from our environment, nor is our environment separate from us."
>
> - William Spear, *Feng Shui Made Easy*

Ener/Chi patterns naturally vary, moving in waves and spirals, ebbs and flows, speeding up where it has the opportunity to move in a straight line as when it shoots down a long hallway, or slowing to a standstill in cluttered or confined spaces. Sharp edges, straight lines and angular corners do not reflect this natural movement of ener/Chi and the result is that we feel more uncomfortable and stressed in highly angular environments. We innately feel more relaxed and at ease the more we incorporate *natural* shapes into our inner spaces, reflecting the soft rounded curves and asymmetrical forms found in nature.

"Living design feels the way homemade bread smells: warm, delicious, and irresistible."

- William Spear

In Feng Shui, our goal is to make rooms inviting so they attract both people *and* ener/Chi. If you do not feel drawn into a particular room, chances are neither will ener/Chi. It is important to be mindful when you arrange things. A good barometer of whether ener/Chi will find it easy to flow freely is to consider whether the location of an object will make it easy or difficult, graceful or awkward for you to move through a space. It can be helpful to walk through your home, imagining yourself moving as the ener/Chi itself does, and notice whether you feel you are able to flow smoothly in and through all areas, or are there places of obstruction, confusion, confinement, stagnation or acceleration?

Ideally, ener/Chi likes to meander around and through your environment like a gentle breeze or trickling stream, nourishing your space with a fresh feeling of aliveness. If ener/Chi flows too quickly it can cause disruption, stress and frustration. If it is too slow it can stagnate resulting in lethargy, depression and disease. When a room is stuffed with too many objects and pieces of furniture, it is helpful to have an abundance of natural light as well as light colored furnishings to aid in balanced ener/Chi flow.

> *"The way that Chi moves through the world is like flowing water, so that when life is going well for us, we can think of ourselves as 'going with the flow'."*
>
> - Gina Lazenby, *The Feng Shui House Book*

Ener/Chi commands our attention and pulls us in certain directions. To identify where ener/Chi is strongest in a particular space, just notice where you are first compelled to move and what you first see. Ener/Chi is another word for vitality. Each room has a different level of need for ener/Chi dependent upon the room's function. With too little ener/Chi, the vitality of an office or exercise room will not motivate us to work hard or inspire creativity to achieve our goals. With too much ener/Chi, the vitality of a bedroom or meditation space will feel chaotic and unsettling, anything but tranquil.

> *"Chi is the universal life force that is found in all living things. It is being created and dissipated all the time. When it is present, the earth smells sweet and everything goes exactly the way you want it."*
>
> - Richard Webster, *Feng Shui for the Workplace*

Mental Flow or "Inner Feng Shui"

"More than those who hate you, more than all your enemies, an undisciplined mind does greater harm."

- Buddha

While many Feng Shui books discuss the benefits of free flowing, balanced environmental ener/Chi, in this book, we add the essential element of mental flow or "Inner Feng Shui" (inner/Chi) to the mix. Inner/Chi is about taking an honest look at your mental, emotional and spiritual roadblocks, those negative, limiting or fear-based thoughts and beliefs that keep you stuck and prevent you from accomplishing your goals. Inner/Chi is essentially the same principle as ener/Chi in your environment, in that your goal is to identify and eliminate areas of stuck, stagnant Chi so that fresh healthy Chi can circulate naturally, restoring vital balance and harmony. With inner/Chi, we look for negative or limiting thoughts and beliefs and take steps to transform and release them, resulting in greater focus, clarity, peace of mind and personal balance.

"We are what our thoughts have made us: so take care about what you think. Words are secondary. Thoughts live; they travel far."

- Swami Vivekananda

Equally significant, in my experience, is that inner/Chi flow is powerfully enhanced by balanced physical well-being resulting from a nutritious diet, adequate rest and regular exercise. While these factors contribute greatly to the flow of inner/Chi when they are present, and detract from it when they are not, aligning one's unique energy flow is very much an "inside job" and a more subtle exercise in personal discipline than physical exercise and diet alone.

> *"And what is balance, but healing? What is healing, but balance?"*
>
> - Kay Gardner, *Music As Medicine*

In addition to nurturing and supporting the needs of a healthy body, enhanced flow, environmental as well as internal, is directly related to increased balance in life. Some significant factors that contribute to a positive personal flow and help keep us balanced mentally, emotionally and spiritually are:

* Nurturing our minds by taking classes, courses and seminars that educate, entertain, empower, and enlighten.

* Nurturing our hearts by tending to the people and relationships in our lives that mean the most to us, and cleaning up any incompletions or miscommunications.

* Nurturing our souls on a daily basis by connecting with Spirit in whatever way is most meaningful. Norman Vincent Peale reminds us to keep our mental and spiritual "contact points" clean so that God can operate through our minds.

> *"Rituals channel your life energy toward the light. Without the discipline of practice, you will tumble constantly backwards into darkness."*
>
> - Lao Tsu, *Philosopher*

As you read through, implement and personally experience the recommended exercises and simple suggestions on the following pages, don't be surprised to find your life taking on a smoother, more harmonious rhythm. Creating an environment that is alive with positive feelings or love and encouragement will support you in unimaginable ways. You are embarking on a journey that just may transform your life. With this book as your guide and free-flowing, balanced ener/Chi as your compass, you can expect to achieve abundant prosperity on all levels.

> *"Your thoughts create your destiny."*
>
> - Suze Orman, *The Courage to Be Rich*

Section One:
The Art of Environmental Flow

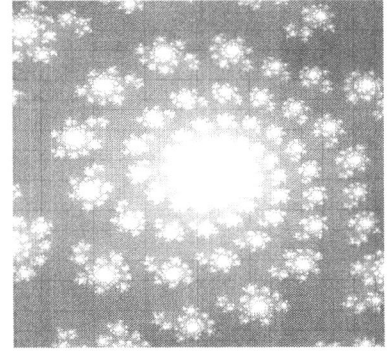

How do You Want Your Life to Be?

> "We were made to enjoy music, to enjoy beautiful sunsets, to enjoy looking at the billows of the sea and to be thrilled with a rose that is bedecked with dew...Human beings are actually created for the transcendent, for the sublime, for the beautiful, for the truthful... and all of us are given the task of trying to make this world a little more hospitable to these beautiful things."
>
> - Desmond Tutu, quoted in The NPR Interviews 1994, edited by Robert Siegel

How do you want your life to look? Successful? Happy? Loving? Healthy? Exciting? Peaceful? Adventurous? Fun? Does it look like that? If not, you may want to ask yourself, why not? One likely explanation may be that your living and working environment does not adequately support you in the achievement of your goals and dreams. You may be wondering how your home or office can have a tangible effect on the level of happiness or success you experience - they're just buildings, inanimate objects, *things*. But are they? Feng Shui recognizes that on one level, *everything* is alive and continually changing, especially in our personal world where everything is *alive* with the memories and associations we give to them. Feng Shui also believes all life is interconnected, that no part of life is isolated from any other part of life. Your health affects your relationships, your relationships affect your career, and your career affects your prosperity and so on. If even one area of your life is in chaos or out of balance, it can potentially affect all other areas of your life, much like when the laundry in your washing machine all shifts to one side during the wash cycle and the entire load is thrown off balance causing the whole works to come to a sudden halt. Feng Shui helps establish balance, clarity, motivation and an overall sense of personal well-being by integrating your personal inner/Chi with the environmental ener/Chi of a particular space.

> *"Be careful what you think, for what you think you will eventually say. Be careful of what you say, for what you say you will eventually do. Be careful about what you do, because your actions will become your habits, and be careful of those habits because your habits will become your destiny."*
>
> - Suze Orman

> *"...generally, balance makes our lives larger and imbalance makes our lives smaller."*
>
> - Clarissa Pinkola Estes, Ph.D.,
>   Women Who Run With the Wolves

Feng Shui = Intention in Physical Form
(getting the most from your rooms by living intentionally)

Practicing Feng Shui helps keep your dreams and goals alive by providing an outward visible means for an inward intention. In other words, environmentally surrounding yourself with your intentions by creating an atmosphere of what I call "intention in physical form."

For example, let's imagine your intention is to increase the amount of money flowing into your life. And let's also imagine that you are willing to *support* this intention by taking whatever *action* necessary to reach your desired goal. To assist you in anchoring your intention in physical form, you decide upon a specific object (Chi enhancer) that personally conveys a sense of wealth, and place it (the "art of placement") in an area where you will see it every day, reminding you of your intention and your willingness to do *whatever it takes* to bring wealth and abundance into your life.

Soon, just as intended, you notice an increase in your cash flow. Do you think that it was the specific Chi enhancer or its precise location/placement that achieved your intention of increased wealth? Or, would you be willing to consider that the object and its location merely *assisted* you, consciously as well as subconsciously, by powerfully reminding you of your intention each time you saw it, reactivating and renewing your commitment to do whatever it takes, and keeping you on course toward achieving your goal? By visually anchoring our intentions in physical form, we create a potent force for accomplishing our goals and transforming our lives.

Each Feng Shui enhancement we implement in our external environment simply acts as a physical reminder. It activates our inner knowing and anchors our intention about what is *really* important to us by keeping it alive in our mind's eye and reminding us what action steps need to be taken next.

Yet, anchoring intentions in physical form with artful, attractive enhancements and placement is only part of the picture. An environmental science like Feng Shui is a powerful tool, but in my experience it is just that - a *tool* - not a *magic bullet*! It is not some mysterious magical formula that, when all your furnishings, objects, elements or directions are all correctly chosen and placed, causes life to automatically run perfectly all by itself. If this were true, wouldn't we already have applied these or similar principles a long time ago and be living the life of our dreams?

While environmental science is a potent tool for positive growth and change, it can only go so far when applied *all by itself*. We must also be willing to work with our inner/Chi as well as our ener/Chi. For example, if you have a limiting belief that you do not deserve wealth or abundance, that belief (inner/Chi) can get in the way of any environmental shifts (ener/Chi). THIS IS KEY! Our inner/Chi can be so effective in creating conflicting intentions, it can literally stop the flow of healthy ener/Chi and keep it from doing its job! Consciously, you may intend to increase your incoming flow of wealth, but subconsciously, you may still have conflicting core beliefs about whether or not you really *deserve* the wealth you desire. This is why it is *essential* to discover your negative or limiting core beliefs and do whatever work necessary to heal and release them.

> *"There is nothing either good or bad,
> but thinking makes it so."*
>
> - William Shakespeare

Your Environment Reflects You!

> "When friends enter a home, they sense its personality and character, the family's style of living - these elements make a house come alive with the sense of identity, a sense of energy, enthusiasm, and warmth, declaring, 'This is who we are; this is how we live.'"
>
> - Ralph Lauren

Your living and working environment (even your car) is a reflection of what is going on inside of you. If you are overly ambitious, overwhelmed, perfectionistic or prone to adopting clutter-bug tendencies in your outer world, it is often a reflection of your inner state of being. It's a two-way street; you affect your environment and your environment affects you. By manipulating your external world, you attract positive change to your internal world.

> "Sometimes what WE want just isn't practical or right for us now. A home with small children SHOULD be set up differently than one with grown children. If you're divorced or remarried and stepchildren visit you often, you'll have to make appropriate arrangements for them. These are not so much questions of lifestyle as of life PASSAGES... An honest home that rings true to the lives of the people who occupy it will always be disarmingly refreshing to visitors."
>
> - Alexandra Stoddard

Live with What You Love

Living surrounded by what we love, creates the atmosphere and energy that we "marinate" in. We know everything that surrounds us is alive with the ener/Chi of the memories, the associations, and the feelings that we give them. Look around your environment and notice what emotions arise as you look at a particular piece of art. Does it evoke a happy memory for you? Maybe you acquired the art at a time in your life you would rather put completely behind you. What about those books you've been meaning to read but now weigh on you as reminders of one more "to do" item on a seemingly endless list of "to do's"? And how about that furniture that you've never really liked, but you think you should hold onto because it was extremely expensive, or some other seemingly-justifiable excuse? Remember, everything you own owns part of you!

> *"Our home becomes a reflection of our inner life...*
> *in the outer."*
>
> - Gunilla Norris, *Journeying in Place*

Here's a little exercise to try that I call my "Chi-depleter" test. When you look at a particular object, notice your physical reaction to it. Specifically notice if you feel a slight sinking or tugging feeling in the general area of your heart. If so, I'd like you to consider that over time, this object is costing you more energy than you can comfortably afford to pay by depleting your precious inner/Chi with repeated daily environmental exposure. It is not contributing to nurturing and uplifting your spirit. Rather, it is draining your inner/Chi, often resulting in depletions in numerous areas of your life, such as finances, relationships and health, far more than you may realize.

Negative Memories

> "I believe my home should be filled with the things that matter to me."
>
> - Oprah Winfrey

After many years of trying to make a very difficult marriage work, I found myself going through the process of a devastatingly painful divorce. I felt overwhelmed with starting my life all over again and dealing with the daunting task of healing the emotional wounds left in the wake of that very toxic relationship.

When the divorce was final, one of the items awarded me from the division of property was what I believed to be a valuable piece of art. I thought since it was so valuable, I "should" hang it in my new home and try to get some use out of it. However, each time I saw that piece of art, it would catapult me right back into reliving those painful memories of the unhappy relationship from which I had just managed to free myself. I took it down from the wall and tried hanging it in another location, thinking that moving it to a different spot might make a difference in my reaction to it. It did not! I eventually realized that having this piece of art in my home, regardless of its perceived value, was costing too much inner/Chi to hold on to it. I needed my home to be a sanctuary, a refuge, and a nurturing, healing place where I could create a brand new life. According to Duncan Phillips, art should be "joy giving and life enhancing" and this old art piece, full of negative memories, didn't fit that description.

Once I realized the hefty price tag of keeping that art piece, it became easy to let it go. I realized that it didn't belong in my new home or my new life. In fact, it wasn't *mine* anymore. After I let it go, I didn't miss it for even one moment. Just the opposite, I felt great relief!

> *"Just don't be surprised to discover that even if what you live with is beautiful, it might no longer suit you."*
>
> - Sarah Ban Breathnach, *Simple Abundance*

This personal story illustrates how important it is to your inner/Chi to *live with what you love*. After hearing that story at one of my Feng Shui seminars in a local bookstore, one woman went home that same evening and began looking at her living room furniture with new eyes. The next morning, she moved all her living room furniture out onto her front lawn and attached a sign that said "Free to a Good Home." By the end of the day, satisfied new owners had claimed every piece! That may be a bit drastic for most of us, but she said it felt great to let go of things she realized she no longer loved.

I've heard it said that "if you want change in your life, move 27 things in your home." While I'm not absolutely sure of the particular significance in the number 27, I do know this advice regularly produces instantaneous shifts! I want to be clear that we are not necessarily talking about big objects here like refrigerators! Following a private consultation, one of my clients, Kristi, decided she would test this philosophy to see if it would help her move through the "stuckness" she had long been experiencing in her career and personal life. One evening, she invested a few minutes "intentionally" rearranging 27 perfume bottles and other vanity items on her powder room counter top. Before long she called with the news of an exciting job opportunity and a budding new relationship. Magic? Or, the result of clarity and focused intention?

> *"Actions create consequences. The intention behind an action determines the consequence. Without action you do not create consequences in the physical world. When you don't know what your intentions are, you are acting unconsciously. Most people act automatically, that's a gentle way of saying they act unconsciously, because they don't know what their intentions are. The consequences that come into your life are those that you create!"*
>
> - Gary Zukov, *The Seat of the Soul*

How is Feng Shui Different from Interior Design?

Have you ever tried to copy decorating ideas you've seen in magazines and implement them in your home only to find that the reality of living with someone else's sense of taste and style didn't really work for you? Feng Shui is about tuning into your own unique soul and asking the questions, "What do I really want? Am I living as I really want to live? Am I living with what I love?" Only by tuning into your true nature can you begin to authentically shape your environment. In *A Home for the Soul*, Anthony Lawler says, "Home should be a place that nurtures the soul. You should get a sense of the life of the people who live in that house and what they really love. By transforming your home in a more soulful way, you become more soulful because your home becomes a means of expressing who you really are and how you really want to live."

The Importance of a Nurturing Atmosphere in Your Environment

"I am fascinated by the way houses make people behave."

- Mary Gordon, *Seeing Through Places*

Since the atmosphere in your home has such an impact on your life, it becomes extremely important to do all you can to create a tranquil, harmonious, loving and nurturing environment. Victoria Moran, author of *Shelter for the Spirit* says that because there are often so many places in our lives where we *don't* have much if any control, like at work or in the outside world, we really need to cherish the one place were we *can* have control, our home. A home that really serves our soul is one in which we recognize ourselves, one where there is evidence of our lives, our habitation and the lives of our family members. Ms. Moran says this goes way beyond interior design and advises, "We need to design the interior of ourselves and let our homes reflect that." It doesn't take an expensive or grand house to shelter your Spirit. A cozy bungalow, a trailer, a studio apartment, even a sailboat, whatever you have can serve beautifully if you realize there is a very special person living there - YOU!

"An interior is the natural projection of the soul."

- Coco Chanel

Catherine Bailly Dunne, author of *Interior Designing for all Five Senses*, writes that decorating your home is all about stimulating your mind and feeding your soul by creating an environment aimed at nurturing your five senses: touch, taste, smell, sight and sound. She claims this technique literally reduces stress. Soft, comfy tactile fabrics for furnishings; warm cheery shades of paint on walls; favorite scented flowers and candles and luscious juicy fruits attractively arranged on your kitchen table trigger pleasant memories. The sounds of your home also represent your everyday life: birds chirping, children playing outside, wind chimes softly tinkling in the breeze, or the relaxing sound of trickling water features. She believes you must *never* underestimate the importance of your home. It fuels your dreams. It gratifies your soul and it energizes you each and every day.

One of Ms. Dunne's most important rules of thumb is that *subtracting is often adding*. This is not always an easy rule to follow because we are often emotionally attached to our furnishings. She recommends enlisting the aid of a trusted friend or professional when dealing with the letting go process, someone who is not attached to your possessions like you are. Someone who can help you remember that letting go of furnishings you no longer need, use, want or love actually seems to make your home sparkle and shine. You become so used to your surroundings that you don't realize that it would actually be less stressful to you if these useless items were eliminated from your environment. It frees you up to let go of things that no longer mirror your soul. As one of my clients happily reported, "Space is the ultimate luxury!"

Creating a loving, supportive environment by surrounding yourself with the things that express your true self, warm your heart, and increase your sense of connectedness with spirit, is absolutely the best gift you can give yourself. It simply boils down to living with *what* you love and loving *where* you live. If you are not giving yourself this precious gift, it's important to understand the reasons *why*. Ask yourself why you're not investing the time and money necessary to create your own "home for the soul," the place were you can truly live and grow physically, emotionally and spiritually, a place that is an essential touchstone for your personal growth and transformation.

> *"How we care for home is a subtle but significant expression of self-esteem."*
>
> - Sarah Ban Breathnach

Sometimes when we begin creating our "home for the soul," it quickly becomes overwhelming. There seems to be so much to be done. A very simple yet powerful tip that can help prevent you from stopping yourself before you even get started is to take the projects or areas you want to work on one-at-a-time. This creates the energy and inspiration of completing one task before moving onto the next, rather than starting on several areas simultaneously. Work on each individual section in bite-size chunks or micro-movements. Just one little baby step at a time will move you forward at a steady pace toward completion.

What Does Balance Feel Like?

Whether we are aware of it or not, to one degree or another, we have all experienced Feng Shui in our lives. For example, think of a time when you entered someone's home for the first time and immediately felt relaxed and welcome in their environment. Their living space just felt great to you yet you really can't explain why. It's not that you necessarily agree with their choices in decorating, you just feel very relaxed and comfortable in their environment. That's an example of how balanced ener/Chi feels. Our consciousness *creates* our environment, and our environment *displays* our consciousness.

Maybe you've noticed that certain stores and shops have a great feeling that literally seems to call out to you to stop in, look around, spend your time and money. Other stores seem almost repellent or leave you feeling depleted; you just can't seem to leave quickly enough!

Have you ever walked into someone's office and immediately noticed you didn't feel at ease in their environment? Maybe you feel anxious to leave, something seems off, and suddenly you don't feel confident about doing business with that person or company anymore. As human beings, we naturally resonate with and are attracted to balanced ener/Chi, and we are uncomfortable around imbalanced ener/Chi and want to move away from it. This is a major reason why Feng Shui is absolutely essential in any environment, personal or professional.

Exercise:

Consider the business environments you most enjoy frequenting. Are they places where you feel at ease and welcome? Are they visually appealing? Is the ambiance attractive and are the employees helpful and friendly? What aspects invite you to linger and spend money in their establishment?

....

....

....

Conversely, think of a time when you felt uncomfortable or even repelled by a business or office environment. Your instincts told you not to do business there but you went against your better judgment. To your dismay (and possible financial disappointment), you realized you should have listened to your instincts in the first place and left before signing on the dotted line.

....

....

....

Does your space fit you?

Samuel Clemens wrote of his house,

> "It had a heart and soul, and eyes to see with; and approvals and solicitudes and deep sympathies; it was of us, and we were in its confidence and lived in its grace and in the peace of its benedictions. We never came home from an absence that it's face did not light up and speak out in eloquent welcome - and we could not enter it unmoved."

Many of us have experienced finding ourselves faced with living or working in environments that aren't right for us. Maybe our space is too dark, too small, too big, too bright, too hot or too drafty. Maybe the ceiling is too low, the neighbors too close, the street traffic too noisy. Often we instinctively know when an environment is not a good fit, but sometimes we choose to live or work there anyway thinking we can find a way to *make it fit*.

At one point in my life, for reasons important at the time, I chose to move halfway across the country to a climate and culture very different from what I'd been accustomed to much of my life. The move happened quickly and the hastily chosen temporary quarters turned out to be far too small, hot and noisy for my personal comfort level. However, I was clear from the start that the accommodations were only temporary. I fully believed I could adequately Feng Shui the space to make it work for what

I thought would be a short period of time. I did everything possible to arrange my ener/Chi (art of placement), adjust my inner/Chi (attitude), clear clutter and work my Bagua map, all in an effort to "Feng Shui my way to happiness." Try as I might, nothing seemed to help. I could find no way to make that space feel like a good "fit" for me. After nearly seven months of dwindling domestic bliss, I finally accepted the only solution left to save sanity was to find a new home as soon as possible.

I had never experienced first hand the dramatically draining effects of living in a "bad fit" space. Just as there are relationships that never seem to be a good fit no matter how hard we try to make them work, the same is true in bad fit environments. The longer we stay in them, the more they sap our energy. The more life force they cost!

When you realize you're in a negative environment (just as with a negative relationship or any situation that doesn't support and nurture your goals and dreams) the best thing you can do for yourself is to make a conscious change. If you keep doing what you've always done, you'll keep getting what you've always gotten. Choose a change you can live with. Baby steps are just fine. But, get in *action* changing things to better suit your needs as soon as you can. *Action* is the key!

"Awareness without action is useless"

- Dr. Phil McGraw, Ph.D., *Life Strategies*

Getting Started with Environmental Feng Shui

"Whether you make your bed in a tiny studio or a sprawling castle, when you've found that place of joy, that's where you can kick off your heels and hang your hat."

- Oprah Winfrey

Let's move on to some specific environmental applications of Feng Shui. First, take the Art of Living Environmental Comfort Survey at the end of this chapter. You can also use the following Environmental Checklist to scan your environment and see where the flow of ener/Chi may be slow or stagnant.

Environmental Checklist

Standing at the entrance to your home or office, imagine seeing it through the eyes of someone who has never been there before and ask yourself:

1. Do you surround yourself only with items you love? Ancient wisdom says: "Everything is talking to you all the time, make sure they have nice things to say." Life is too short to live with things you don't like. Consider donating anything you no longer love to a friend or to charity. In doing so, you'll be well on your way to creating the ultimate luxury, space!

2. Do you get a peaceful feeling within your living space? Your environment, including your office or workspace, should reflect a sense of safety. It should be the one place in the world where you can always rely on feeling relaxed and supported.

3. Does your environment look or feel cluttered? Clutter can cause Chi to slow down and stagnate. Your life will begin to reflect a corresponding stuckness the longer you live in a cluttered environment. Eliminate as much clutter as you can. Try to keep your environment clean and orderly.

4. Even though your environment may be small, does it give the *impression* of space? Mirrors are highly effective in creating an illusion of more space.

5. Are your entrances entrancing? Refresh entry ways, *especially* the one you use most often (even if it is only the laundry room door used to come and go from the garage) by adding welcoming elements such as fresh flowers or painting the walls with cheery, warm colors like buttercup yellow or blushing peach - any color that feels rejuvenating and uplifting to you.

6. Does your environment have sufficient natural lighting to give a sense of lightness, warmth and welcome? This is especially important for entryways where adequate lighting is an essential ingredient in creating an uplifting, inviting feeling. Are any areas dark, gloomy or un-welcoming? You can increase the effect of *natural* lighting by adding full-spectrum bulbs in place of fluorescents or regular light bulbs whenever possible.

7. Is your color scheme attractive to you personally? If you do not live with colors you love, you'll never feel completely at home in your space. For example, if you love cool colors like purple and blue, you'll never feel completely at home with warm tones like orange and yellow. If your environment has an abundance of cool, white-tone walls and furniture or decor, warm the area up by bringing in rugs, throw cushions, and wall hangings in any

shade of red from pale pink to rich purple. Animal skins, even faux animal skins add the element of fire and warmth to a room.

8. Is your space enhanced with art works that hold meaning for you? Choose art that makes your heart sing - whimsical, beautiful, colorful, peaceful, or dramatic. (Helpful tip: it is better to live with blank walls until you can live with that which you truly love!)

9. Does your space please your sense of smell? Use aromatic, deliciously scented potpourri to create a warm and fragrantly inviting atmosphere. Choose dried flower petals scented with fresh citrus, sensuous vanilla or any fragrance you especially enjoy. Remember to change out any dried or silk potpourri or floral arrangements when they begin looking dead. The rule of thumb with Chi enhancers is, "If they look dead, *they are dead.*"

10. What does your environment sound like? Soft, pleasing music, tinkling wind chimes or gurgling water features create the sensation of circulating Chi in the form of sound. (Helpful tip: Your bedroom may not be the best place for a water feature as the sound of running water may increase the tendency for nighttime trips to the bathroom!)

11. Can you see the main entrance to the room from your bed, your desk or anywhere you normally sit and relax, without turning your head more than 45 degrees? Being in the "command position" allows you to see the door even in your peripheral vision and prevents the occurrence of being unnecessarily startled. You will feel more protected and supported having a clear view of the main entrance.

12. Pay attention to living "Chi enhancers." Bring in fresh, vibrant Chi with healthy, live plants or "life-like" silk plants. Take consistently loving good care of all pets. If pets are not well loved, healthy, and happy, they can actually become Chi-*depleters*.

13. Does your plumbing have any leaks? Make sure all plumbing is in good working order in all areas: bathrooms, kitchens, laundry rooms, etc. You don't want any unplanned energy "drains" anywhere, symbolically or otherwise.

14. Are there any areas you find especially unattractive to look at? For example, many of us have "cord nests," those unsightly tangled mounds of wires and cords that seem to multiply behind electronic equipment. Or, does your environment suffer from sharp or extreme angles that would feel much more relaxing if they were softened up a bit? For example, large angular curtainless windows benefit by having sharp edges softened with rods swathed in luscious fabrics in a swag-like manner.

Clutter

> "Every square inch counts. There is no such thing as a place to hide stuff."
>
> - Terah Katherine Collins, *The Western Guide to Feng Shui*

Think for a moment about the environment you work in: office, studio, cubicle, station, workshop, even your car, whatever type of space it happens to be. Is it as organized as you would like it to be or does it fall short of the mark? Often those who think their workspace is not very organized are actually organized fairly well because they are always striving to improve. It's those of us who think we've pretty much got our clutter handled that rationalize our disorganization with thoughts like, "What's wrong with a little clutter? At least, I know where everything is!" My intention and hope is that the more you learn about clutter the more you'll never look at it the same way again!

> "Any inharmony on the external indicates there is mental inharmony."
>
> - Florence Scovel Shinn, *The Game of Life*

A disorganized or messy environment blocks the flow of healthy, balanced ener/Chi. In an organized, tidy environment, energy circulates freely and distributes its beneficial effects in all areas. But when clutter impedes its normal flow, ener/Chi becomes blocked, stuck and stagnant, affecting all who live and work in these often chaotic areas. They may notice a lower physical energy level, inhibited creativity, lack of clarity and focus in their thinking process, and basic diminished effectiveness in anything they try to accomplish. This phenomenon is easily visible in any room of the house. It is more difficult to cook creatively and spontaneously in a disorganized kitchen or read and absorb knowledge as effectively at an unkempt desk. Even one's sleep can be adversely affected in a messy bedroom. Author Gunilla Norris advises it's better to have less than to have a lot because clutter in our homes "makes clutter in our heads."

It's important to be clear about the type of clutter I'm referring to here. I am not referring to stuff you may have a lot of but which is useful or brings you joy. I'm referring to things you don't really need, use, love or that don't serve a purpose in your life anymore and maybe never did. Anything that is unfinished, incomplete, unused or unworn for a year or more is also very likely in the clutter category.

> *"Clutter in your thinking, manifests as clutter in your environment."*
>
> - Florence Scovel Shinn

Keeping your home clean is one of the easiest and most effective ways to balance and refresh your home's environmental Chi. A dirty or dusty environment, just like clutter, keeps stagnant energy in your living space and is almost always an indication of a lack of healthy ener/Chi circulation, which can also create blocked mental and emotional states such as confusion, depression and frustration.

Another unhappy side-effect of clutter is that it can contribute to a variety of health challenges often manifesting as weight gain, decreased physical stamina, clogged complexions and even clogged arteries. One clue to discovering where clutter is most problematic is to look for areas that appear dingy or dusty, feel heavy or claustrophobic, or smell musty and stale. Clearing the clutter away in any stagnant areas by sorting and purging as well as thoroughly cleaning will give your environment a jump-start and attract vital new life force.

> *"As within, so without. And, as without, so within."*
>
> - Florence Scovel Shinn

Incomplete Cycles of Action

Clutter is often the result of incompletion. Incompletions are many times the stagnant energy behind procrastination. Another way of looking at clutter is that it is energy you have no access to because it is still tied up in the things you *intended* to do, and some part of your consciousness is still tracking those intentions. Many of us have even gone so far as to train our consciousness to *justify* that it's okay for us to do this. The truth is, if we are procrastinating, we probably still have our energy tied up in "incompletes," no matter how we try to justify it.

Completing "cycles of action" by completing unfinished projects or even just tossing them out, frees up massive energy, contributing generously to your personal inner/Chi and spiritual ecology. Because everything you own, *owns part of you!* Learn to be very selective about *where* you invest your energy.

> *"Our life is frittered away by detail.*
> *Simplify, Simplify, Simplify."*
>
> - Henry David Thoreau

De-cluttering Techniques

It has been said that *mess is stress!* Mess stresses your life in ways you may not even be aware of. One client wisely said, "When my things are disorganized, my life is disorganized!" Can you remember a time when unnecessary stress set the tone for your day with the discovery that you'd misplaced your car keys? Your stress level soared as you lost precious time in your frantic misplaced key search, trying to beat the clock and not be late to work, miss your airplane flight or that once-in-a-lifetime opening night curtain call? Experts estimate that we lose millions of dollars every year replacing items that we cannot find, items lost in the chaos of our own clutter.

Feeling overwhelmed when you begin clutter clearing is not unusual. You may even find yourself thinking that this clutter clearing wasn't such a great idea after all! When, in truth, you are on the verge of creating clarity out of chaos if you just stay the course, one bite-size chunk at a time. Being overwhelmed can actually be a crucial step in the clutter clearing process. It is definitely not the time to give up!

> "How can we focus our attention on what's truly important when we're half-crazed because we can never find anything?"
>
> - Sarah Ban Breathnach

Clutter clearing is often emotionally charged because many of us feel barriers or blocks to letting go of our stuff. We all have good reasons for why we want to hang on. Sometimes we keep things for sentimental reasons because they remind us of a special time in our past. Other times we keep things we no longer have any use for because we paid a lot for them and we don't feel we can just give them away. Or maybe we got a real bargain on something, or we think it's such a one-of-a-kind item, all seemingly good reasons for keeping stuff we don't really need or use, and maybe don't even want any longer.

Some people feel they need to have an abundance of stuff around them to create a sense of security and comfort. Each of us has our own personal comfort level for how much stuff is enough stuff. One way to recognize your own personal comfort level is to notice whether you feel you have so much that it is intimidating to even look through it all. If so, you'll never enjoy any of it and it will become a burden rather than a benefit.

Organizing and clutter clearing isn't just about throwing things out, says Julie Morgenstern, author of *Organizing from the Inside Out*. It's really about identifying what things are most important to you and making those items easily accessible. Clutter clearing and getting organized is actually quite liberating and empowering. Staying organized and out of "clutter chaos" is a great way to nurture yourself. You are able to make the most of your talents, skills and rich resources in your life as well as be at your personal best when you have exactly the things you need close at hand.

In her helpful book, *Organizing from the Inside Out*, Ms. Morgenstern uses the term SPACE as an acronym to describe her unique process. Here's a brief summary:

S = SORT

Pick one room at a time and only one section of that room to sort through. Don't allow yourself to zigzag all over the house, working on unrelated areas willy-nilly. Avoid disbursing your clutter clearing efforts by spreading yourself too thin. Concentrate on one area at a time.

P = PURGE

Stay within the same space you just sorted, purge (toss out) everything you no longer need, want or love. For those items that you want to give a home to and keep in another area, have a "goes elsewhere" box to put them in so you don't have to leave the space you're currently working in and risk getting distracted.

A = ASSIGN A HOME

Decide where you want to put the items you're keeping. For example, what drawer, what shelf, which end of the pole in your closet will best suit how you will use the item? Assign your items a home and put them away after each use.

C = CONTAINERIZE

As you assign homes and put things away, it will become obvious what kind of additional containers you need for storage, baskets, plastic bins, boxes, etc. Containerizing is key because once everything has it's own "home," it becomes much easier to keep things put away and organized after every use.

E = EQUALIZE

Since the one thing in life we can count on is change, daily maintenance and periodic tune-ups are necessary to keep your system current. If a room is organized, it should take no longer than three to five minutes at the end of the day to straighten up, because everything now has a home.

Clutter Clearing Tips

Here are a few tips to help make your clutter clearing more effective:

1. Pace yourself. Don't attempt to take on the entire garage in one day, or go on a clutter clearing blitz in that over-stuffed spare bedroom that has somehow become the "junk" room. It may even be too much to take on an entire closet at one time. Micro-movements are the *key* to your clutter clearing success.

2. Start with baby steps. Maybe just one box at a time and it's okay if it's only a *small* box. Remember that it is your *intention* to make clutter clearing a regular part of your housekeeping routine that will create the balanced flow of vital, new ener/Chi.

3. Don't give up anything you're not *ready* to part with!

4. Begin with what you *know* you can live without. Don't get too ruthless too fast. It's *not necessary* to throw out *everything* you haven't used in the past year. In fact, it is not a good idea to throw out anything you're not really ready to let go of. Look for things you know you won't miss because they haven't been an active part of your life for a long time and keep the things you truly love.

5. If you forgot you even had it, DON'T KEEP IT! Unless you can find an immediate use for something you forgot you had, it's time to toss it. Don't look for reasons to justify keeping the incredible one-of-a-kind bargain you bought six years ago and forgot all about because you really didn't have a use for it then and still don't now!

6. There is a strong connection between possessions and opportunities, between hanging onto the old and how much new you're willing to let come into your life. When you have too much stuff you don't need or use, fewer opportunities can come in to your life because there is less space for them to occur. Feel free to chant as your new clutter-clearing mantra: "*Space is my ultimate luxury.*"

7. It's been said that if we desire more abundance in our lives we must create a *vacuum* to attract the good we seek. When you let go of the things you no longer need, use, want, or love, you are freeing up energy to attract your heart's desire because *now* you have space in your life for those desires to manifest. How can more good come to you if you haven't taken even a little time to create room in your life by making a dent in your clutter pile? Here's a great tip: Set your intention to let go of anything you currently do not have a use for, anything you are ready to let go of or anything you no longer love. Then, set your timer for 30 minutes and begin sorting and clearing. When the timer goes off and the 30 minutes are up, you'll have the choice whether to set the timer for another 30 minutes and continue clutter clearing, or to move on to another task for the day. Either

way, you will have created a shift in the stuck energy previously held in that clutter. Sorting and purging clutter, even for only 30 minutes at a time, is a powerful step in releasing and re-circulating stagnant, trapped ener/Chi.

8. Taking care of the "little things" that have been piling up for weeks or months, such as bills, letters or emails creates a sense of completion that frees up your ener/Chi and helps you gain a renewed sense of clarity and motivation. Helpful tip: What task comes to mind that you could easily complete today?

9. Try to avoid getting side tracked with zigzag organizing. Don't stop to fill out that long-lost warranty when you're clearing your desktop. Put it in your "to do" pile for your next "to do" time allotment.

10. Create a "dumping" drawer specifically for your keys, coins, wallet, etc., keeping everything corralled in one spot, rather than being strewn across the dresser or the counter top.

11. If you haven't used that shampoo, spray, lotion, etc., within the last three to six months, you probably never will. Toss it out!

12. Beware of impulse buying. If you don't know how, where or when you will use that special purchase, don't buy it! You may be purchasing clutter!

Specific Applications

Let's explore some more Feng Shui applications for specific areas like entrances, bathrooms, kitchens, bedrooms and offices as well as usage of color, plants and mirrors.

Entrances

> "If you have it, you don't need to have anything else; and if you don't have it, it doesn't matter much what else you have."
>
> - Sir James M. Barrie, English playwright, writing about charm in 1907.

Entrances should be *entrancing*, giving the very first impression of who we are in our home. Within moments after entering a new environment, we intuitively know if it has charm or comfort for us.

Do you feel beckoned to sink into the room's comfortably cozy, cheerful ambiance? Do you sense harmony, serenity, hospitality, and spontaneous touches of whimsy, simple beauty or even nurturing energy? Entryways give the very first impression of a space so it is especially important to pay particular attention to creating a warm sense of welcome. Fresh flowers, lush plants, a small gurgling water fountain, uplifting art, a sparkling crystal chandelier/light fixture or soft, natural lighting are all excellent choices as entryway greeters, giving an indication of the warmth that waits within.

> "Why do we love certain houses, and why do they seem to love us? It is the warmth of our individual hearts reflected in our surroundings."
>
> - T.H. Robsjohn-Gibbings

The structural front door of your home is considered the "main mouth" of Chi and as such is responsible for a good deal of the harmonious flow of energy into and out of any environment, whether that door is actually your main entrance door or not. Outside, it is important to make sure the approach or walkway to the main door is clean, clearly visible and easily accessible. Prune back or eliminate spiky, thorny plants that may give an unwelcoming "stay away" message. Trim overgrown plants and clear away anything else that may be impeding the smooth flow of fresh, vital Chi toward the main entry.

Gates can be a wonderful asset for creating a fresh mind-set upon entering a new space. They can literally change your thought process by giving you the opportunity to pause mentally between where you are and where you want to go. Garden gates don't need to be elaborate to be effective, an opening in a hedge can be a gate in itself. A pair of posts, one on either side of the front walk, can establish a simple threshold, a subtle landmark defining the boundary between public and private space.

The more you personalize this threshold; paint the posts robins-egg blue, plant pansies around the base or install a romantic trellis with climbing blossoms, the more you will be introducing clues that entice one to the welcome that waits within. The design of the gate is limited only by your imagination and by the appropriateness with which it complements your home. Ornate wrought iron, carved oak, classic picket... what style best expresses the character of your yard or garden? If the garden or yard is small, consider attaching a weather-proof mirror or other reflective surface to the inside of a wooden gate, which acts like a window, reflecting, extending and enlarging the small space within. Whenever possible, make sure the gate opens *into* the garden, rather than out, so it *invites* your guests inward. A few pots of bright blossoms, a garden bench just inside the gate and whimsical stepping-stones repeat the welcoming invitation to enter and relax.

> *"Oh, the fun of arriving at a house and feeling the spark that tells you that you were going to have a good time.*
>
> - Mark Hampton

The Importance of Color

Colors have a language all their own. Some colors are bold and aggressive while others are soothing and sensual. Some colors are nondescript, making no particular statement at all. Still others feel intentionally sterile as in many hospitals and doctor's offices, creating a sense of consummate professionalism and confidence.

When we think of the colors we would like to have in our environment, the colors we want to marinate ourselves in day in and day out, we need look no further than our all time favorites. Maybe you've always been partial to bright purple, electric fuchsia or lime green, but think those tones might become a bit much to live with on a day to day basis. True, an entire room or even one wall painted such a dominant shade might be too intense. However, consider exploring the creative options for enhancing your environment with small but effective focal points in these favorite colors, i.e. art, lighting, or unique furniture.

For example, one of my client's favorite shades had always been purple but an entire purple living room would have been just too much for her to live with everyday. She opted to paint her walls a soft, eggshell white subtly tinted with a few drops of a rich purple hue blended in at the paint store. Now her walls give the perfect backdrop to her couch's purple accent pillows giving her favorite purple art pieces and the room a uniquely warm, inviting feeling without being overpowering.

If your preference leans toward cooler, more calming colors, choose those with no red tone at all such as pure blues or greens. However, just as with too much of a warm color, like orange or red dominating a room, the same can be true of cool tones. An easy solution to bring in balance is to apply a color of an opposite hue. For example, if your room has predominantly true-blue cool tones (blue with no red) bring in a warm shade you especially like, such as any color with some shade of red in it, from pale peach to bright orange or even vibrant eggplant. Or, if a room is a contrast in stark, high-tech white and black, bringing in even one accent piece in a warm tone, like a bright poppy red vase, a favorite painting, unique pottery or accent pillows can make all the difference in taking the room from interesting to sensational!

Plants

Healthy, lush, large-leafed plants bring in vibrant outdoor energy. This is essential because the more time we spend indoors, the more we are removed from the "natural world." Bringing in living greenery effectively helps make the connection between the natural world and the man-made world. However, sickly, prickly or puny plants actually deplete our ener/Chi sending out a non-verbal message that is not necessarily healthy, positive or uplifting. Be sure to replace any less-than-vibrant plants with new large-leafed, robust ones.

Lush green plants provide an excellent way to bring in nourishing ener/Chi and fresh oxygen. Healthy plants have a naturally uplifting effect on us emotionally and mentally as well as physically. When selecting plants, the rounder or fuller the leaves, the better. Sharp, sword-like leaves symbolically give the message to "stay away." They're not as friendly, warm and inviting as large-leafed plants.

Be sure to choose plants that are a good match for the available lighting in your environment. For example, if your home receives a great deal of sun, make sure you choose plants that can handle full sun. And vice versa. If your house has more indirect or subdued lighting, choose plants that have equivalent lower lighting requirements. Your local plant store can answer any questions you have in selecting just the right plants for your particular environment.

Most important, if you do not enjoy the responsibility of the maintenance and upkeep living plants require, if it is more of a burden than a pleasure to you, you can create a very similar effect with virtually no maintenance worries by choosing healthy, realistic looking, large-leafed silk plants. Just remember that silk has a definite life span, usually about one year. After that time, it may require a good washing or replacement. The rule of thumb is: if silk plants begin to look dead, they are dead! Toss them out and bring in vibrant new ener/Chi with fresh silk plants.

Ornamental bamboo is a plant that is enjoying increasing popularity in the United States and is believed to be a symbol of good luck, bestowing harmony and success in all areas of life to its fortunate owners. "Lucky Bamboo" (*Dracaena sanderana*) has long been sold by Asian nursery owners and gardeners in Southern California, but has recently become trendy in many areas of the United States because it is often recommended as a Feng Shui Chi enhancer. A local schoolteacher told me she likes what lucky bamboo stands for: harmony, prosperity and good fortune, and says she feels it gives her a more positive outlook on life. However, one Los Angeles plant importer believes the only real luck the plant has is its ability to grow under virtually any circumstances - they never die!

Mirrors

Mirrors are excellent for correcting a variety of "Chi-challenged" situations. One of their primary benefits is activating and uplifting the ener/Chi while enlarging any space. Consider places where we often see large mirrors: gyms, exercise rooms, dance studios and department stores, very busy, active places. Mirrors are wonderful for doubling our experience of "aliveness" by reflecting our ener/Chi right back at us.

However, there are some environments where increasing the energy is not especially desirable, for example, bedrooms. This doesn't mean that you should not have mirrors in your bedroom. It only means that it's a good idea to assess how well you are sleeping at night when determining whether removing large mirrors would be helpful in calming the energy of the room. If you are not sleeping very well, it is a good idea to find ways to calm down the space rather than invigorate it with mirrored Chi enhancers.

One of my clients, Lori is married to a highly successful CEO of his own corporation. During our consultation, Lori told me that her husband Sam often had difficulty sleeping through the night. It wasn't unusual to find him in the garage at two or three in the morning working on his prized Harley, a rewarding and fun pastime for him but not especially conducive to getting up early the next morning. When we entered their master bedroom suite, I noticed one entire wall was covered with floor-to-ceiling mirrored closet doors and, not coincidentally, on the same side of the room as Sam's side of the bed. I suggested to Lori that it would be a good idea to calm down the ener/Chi of the room as much as possible so Sam could relax more easily into deep, restful sleep.

Lori's side of the bed led to romantic French doors, framed by lovely, sheer drapes. I suggested she purchase complementary drapes that could be mounted over the mirrored closet doors as if they were also a set of French doors. Lori managed to find fabric that was nearly a perfect match and commissioned drapes made to be hung over the closet mirrors. Soon after the "mirror-drapes" were installed, an astonished and relieved Lori called with the happy news that Sam had been sleeping soundly through the night ever since.

This is a very simple solution or "cure" and one that can be accomplished relatively inexpensively, especially when compared with the option of changing out the mirrored closet doors to a non-mirrored surface. Lori chose a more high-end solution by having her mirror-drapes custom-made. However, a simple version of mirror-drapes can be easily created with sheets in a shade matching your bedspread or room decor, hung from a bamboo pole or shower rod. Feel free to be as creative and clever as your time and budget will allow.

Another benefit of mirrors is that they are an excellent tool for making small spaces appear much larger than they really are by giving the illusion of "disappearing" walls and opening up small areas. Also, mirrors are great for effectively brightening a dark room and bringing more of the outdoors *inside*. By hanging a mirror on a wall opposite an existing window where it catches and reflects natural light, you will greatly increase the aliveness of any room.

A useful tip when selecting mirrors is to avoid antiqued, cracked, cloudy or layered mirrors that create an unclear, shattered or distorted reflection. A beveled edge around the perimeter of the mirror is fine. When it comes to mirrors the simpler, the better.

Kitchens

Have you ever noticed that when you have guests in your home, everyone gathers in the kitchen? Ask any real estate agent and they will tell you that kitchens are at the top of the list as one of the most important areas for any new home buyers. Kitchens are literally the heart of a home. It is essential that everything be in proper working order to support the life-sustaining function of this primary piece of your home's anatomy. Your faucet and sink need to work properly with no leaks, your refrigerator must maintain desired temperatures and all the burners on your stove need to function well.

There is a traditional Feng Shui belief that your kitchen stove is a symbol of prosperity in your home. Not only is it essential that your stove is in good working order, it is also thought that placing a mirror behind the stove in such a way as to reflect the burners, doubles the appearance of the burners, thereby doubling your wealth. While it would be difficult to prove that the addition of a mirror actually doubles your wealth, it is easy to see that this simple enhancement increases a sense of greater space and freedom by seemingly "disappearing" the wall over the stove and creating the illusion of a window rather than solid wall.

Another benefit is that the mirrored reflection allows the cook to see what's going on behind them while facing the stove, preventing any "startling" or unexpected surprises. If you have enough room above your stove, give it a try and see how a mirror can enlarge and brighten an otherwise small space.

Another helpful tip for kitchens is to take a good look at just how effectively the existing space is being used. For example, how many junk drawers do you think you have? Or maybe I should ask, how many junk drawers do you think you *need*? I think it is absolutely fine and probably essential to have one junk drawer in your kitchen, but try to keep it to just one! The trick is to periodically sort, purge, and keep it as organized as possible, so you know exactly what lives in there. Because somehow, when you're not looking, those junk drawers seem to breed and before you know it, you'll have six of them!

Bathrooms

Symbolically, toilets, sink and tub drains are considered *potential drains* to your financial resources. Whenever possible, keep toilet seat lids down and bathroom doors closed. Where your attention goes, energy flows. Above all, make sure the plumbing is in good working order and repair any leaks immediately. It is also preferable to avoid having your desk in your workplace next to or in view of the bathroom. If there is no alternative, keep the bathroom door closed and place a decorative mirror on the outside of the door. This will anchor your intention to retain your resources as well as reflect away those situations that may unnecessarily drain resources from you.

A great way to balance the watery feeling prevalent in most bathrooms and give a sense of thriving Chi is to place a healthy green plant on the top of the toilet tank. Remember to match your plant to the existing lighting requirements and keep it well nourished. Pothos are quite hardy and grow well under many difficult lighting conditions.

Bedrooms

Jane and her partner had been experiencing difficulty in their love life for some time. During our consultation, I suggested that bedrooms are for rest and intimacy, not for work. Jane realized that having her computer in their bedroom was actually creating the ener/Chi of conflicting intentions. When she was working at her computer, she felt like her bed was inviting her to lie down and take a nap. When she would lie down to sleep or enjoy intimacy with her mate, it seemed her computer was nagging her to get up and work on yet another project. She decided to move the computer workstation out of the bedroom and in its place put a petite, favorite table with candles framing a romantic wall hanging. She noticed that just this small change created a more romantic, intimate feeling in the bedroom and an improvement in the closeness she felt with her sweetheart.

In my experience, bedrooms are best suited for intimacy and relaxation. If you are having difficulty sleeping, check to see if your bedroom is being used for non-restful activities, such as exercising, office work, paying bills, even watching television can sometimes be considered a less than relaxing activity. I've heard it said that rooms *remember* everything that happens in them, so if you've been doing non-restful activities all day in your bedroom, when you go to bed at night you risk bringing all that energy to bed with you. If you like to watch television while lying in your bed, you are inviting the whole world in with you, including the bad news! Make your bedroom into a snugly, cozy, "nesting" area. It's also a good idea to make it as dark and quiet as possible when you're sleeping. Window treatments, and even in some cases, separate curtains or coverings for large mirrors (like closet doors) are quite helpful for keeping out reflected light and increasing restful ener/Chi.

Bedroom Tips

1. To enhance a sense of security and protection in your bedroom, position your bed so you can see the main entrance or doorway while lying down. If the only workable placement for your bed does not allow this, position a standing mirror so that it reflects the doorway in such away as to be seen from your bed.

2. To create a more restful, peaceful feeling, keep the area under the bed clean and clear. Try not to use this under-bed space as a dumping ground or storage area for stuff that often serves to clog the energy in the bedroom. If you absolutely must use your under-bed space for storage, do your best to keep the items neatly organized. No chaotic junk drawers, bins or containers, please!

3. Placing your bed's headboard against a wall helps create a sense of being grounded and securely backed up. This gives a feeling of being supported as you sleep and is especially important if your bed has no headboard. Beware of heavy or stacked bookcase headboards

that allow a great deal of weight to be stacked over your head as you sleep. It is all too common to find these in homes where headaches or sinus pressure are problematic. The same thing goes for heavy wall art hanging over the head of the bed. The heavier the wall hanging, the more pressure those sleeping underneath may experience. Even though our rational, conscious mind knows that the heavy picture hanging over the head of our bed has been securely bolted to the wall, our primitive, emotionally-reactive subconscious mind will continue its job of being paranoid about whether it might someday fall down on us.

To the subconscious mind, our home represents a place of security, a haven for rest and rejuvenation from the chaotic world. Any threat, whether perceived or real, disturbs this precious balance of rest and rejuvenation. For example, a heavy bookcase headboard does not in and of itself cause headaches, sinus pressure or neck and shoulder pain. The heavy bookcase merely acts as a trigger for an individual's perpetual subconscious anticipation that the books may eventually topple over, leaving their neck and shoulder muscles locked in chronic gridlock in expectation of a potential avalanche. To rest easy, it is far safer and more reassuring to decorate with "soft" art, like hanging tapestries, silk flower wall arrangements, or sheer, flowing fabric canopies draped swag-like over your bed. Use your imagination — the sky's the limit! Create a uniquely personalized nesting space that nurtures relaxation, rest and intimacy.

4. If your intimate relationship is not as hot as you'd like (or possibly non-existent), try spicing things up in the bedroom with any color from the "red" family, from pale peach to deep, rich eggplant. You may want to go wild and paint your entire bedroom in rich, warm hues. Or you may simply choose to add touches of your favorite "warm tone" color with specific accent pieces of "romantic art" (preferably things in pairs that give a sense of loving and intimacy). These symbolically anchor your intention to create the quality of romance and intimacy you desire. A good rule of thumb in choosing your sheets and overall tone of your bedroom decor is to select a healthy balance of warm tones (reds) vs. cool tones (blues and greens). Cool tones are often associated with cooling down passion. Also, look for sheets that feel yummy to your skin, such as satin, high thread count cotton, or jersey T-shirt sheets. The goal is to create a sensual space that makes bedtime something you look forward to every single night.

Offices

Just as your home environment reflects who you are, so does your office. Is your office a joy to work in each day? Does it accurately represent you to your clients? What does it tell them about you? Does it convey the caliber of service they can expect you to deliver? Is your office easy to locate from the street with adequate parking facilities. Is the main entrance clean, well-marked and businesslike, yet welcoming? Or, is the signage inadequate and the entrance difficult to park near or locate? Is the reception area comfortable and well maintained, with a feeling similar to that of a comfortable living room? Or is it sterile, poorly lit or uninviting? Is your personal office space neat, organized, warm and attractive, yet professional? Or is it cluttered, chaotic, dirty, disorganized and maybe even stuffy? It doesn't take a rocket scientist to figure out which office environment is most enjoyable and conducive to successful business transactions for you and your clients.

> *"Clutter gets in the way of clarity and clarity is the gateway to financial freedom."*
>
> - Suze Orman

Let's take a closer look at how our offices give subtle and not so subtle messages to our clients. Think about the non-essential office ener/Chi enhancers you choose to surround yourself with: knick-knacks, decor, or objects d'art. What do these personal items tell others about you and do they accurately represent who you truly are? One particular client's office ener/Chi enhancements seemingly reflected his softer side. On the wall, behind his desk, hung a collection of ornate, one-of-a-kind, antique hats. The message they gave wasn't exactly clear, especially since these were ladies hats! Interestingly, one of his biggest challenges was convincing potential clients that he could be aggressive and tenacious enough to take on and accomplish the high-level corporate projects he was bidding for. Another client had a collection of ice hooks, picks and ice axes on his office wall. Interesting? Maybe interesting to another ice hook, pick or ice axe collector, but in general, not the most inviting choice for his primary clientele. A client greeted by so many pointy, sharp edges could find themselves feeling a bit on edge! Or, they might get the *point* that doing business with you is not such a *sharp* idea! Is it beginning to make sense how the arrangement and enhancement of your office can effectively contribute to making or breaking your career?

In offices, especially those with open workstations, we're often presented with a great deal of simultaneous stimulation. Ideally, we want to create a sense of balance in our work area that feels not too open and not too closed. One cure for decreasing the feeling of chaos often created by several open workstations in one large area is to incorporate room dividers between each station as well as behind the client's seating area facing the workstation. Now, when a client enters the space and has the support of a partition behind them, they experience a feeling of *protection*. This simple solution makes it easier for them to focus on the business at hand.

"If you wish to be rich, you must be orderly. All men with great wealth are orderly and order is heavens first law!"

- Florence Scovel Shinn

Helpful Office Tips

1. Whenever possible, never sit with your back facing the door. Always try to position your desk and chair in the "command position" with a view of the main entrance to your work area. A clear view of the door helps you feel more secure and promotes greater productivity.

2. Limit the amount of time spent under fluorescent lighting, which depletes ener/Chi, leaving you feeling sluggish and drained by the end of the day.

3. Rounded corners and edges on desks, tables, walls, etc. are always preferable. Try to keep sharp cornered objects to a minimum and whenever possible, softened or disguised by lush, large-leafed plants.

4. Green plants are wonderful for bringing in vibrant ener/Chi as they help bring the outdoors inside. Choose healthy plants with full, rounded leaves that match the lighting requirements of your office and keep them well nourished.

5. A lower maintenance option for bringing the outdoors in is the use of posters or artwork depicting the great outdoors or "window art" that gives the illusion of looking out a window onto a beautiful scene.

6. Bringing in "fire" tones (any shade with the color red in it from pale peach to vibrant eggplant) serves to balance the starkness of cool white or beige tone walls often present in abundance in professional environments as well as the rigidity of metal office furniture and equipment.

7. If you work out of your home, try to keep your working and living areas separate. This may be difficult if you live in a studio apartment, but it can be done. One idea is to face your desk in such a way, that when sitting at your desk, your bed is out of your line of sight. This is especially helpful if your desk can be positioned near a window with a pleasant view helping to create the illusion of working in a separate office space outside of your home.

8. Arrange a screen or room divider around your desk to conceal it and any office equipment from sight. That way when you're working, it becomes easier to focus without being distracted by the personal living space of your apartment. And when you are not working, your office area can be made virtually invisible so you can enjoy your leisure time without constantly being reminded of all the work you *could* be doing.

Summary of Environmental Tips

1. Eliminate or reduce clutter effectively reducing chaos and balancing environmental ener/Chi.

2. Make entrances *entrancing*!

3. Keep all living things in your environment lovingly cared for, including plants, pets and relationships.

4. Jettison anything that stirs up negative memories. Live with what you love and love what you live with.

5. Surround yourself with colors that complement and uplift you!

6. Strategic usage of healthy greenery and outdoor artwork effectively brings the *natural* world into your man-made world.

7. Mirrors help activate and enlarge the ener/Chi in any space.

8. Make sure all plumbing is maintained in good working order.

9. Kitchens are the heart of our homes. It is essential that everything be in proper working order and clutter free in this central gathering place.

10. Keep the focus of your bedroom on intimacy, relaxation, and a place to rejuvenate and let go of your cares.

11. By choosing the "command position" at your desk, you will feel more in control and eliminate unnecessary surprises from someone unexpectedly coming up behind you.

By following these simple suggestions, you are implementing a surefire method of attracting, creating and maintaining flow and balance in your environment, your *outward* Feng Shui. In the next chapter, we'll explore ideas and easy techniques for enhancing your *inward* Feng Shui… bringing harmony, prosperity and peace to your life from the inside out! But first, I invite you to take the Environmental Comfort Survey on the following pages.

> *"Wind chimes and crystals hung in exactly the right places may increase the possibility of changing our perceptions through the change in our environment, but we would be wise to remember that self-development begins within and will really only be supported by what occurs in the external world."*
>
> – William Spear

The Art of Living Environmental Comfort Survey (ECS)

1. Clutter	Regardless of the size of your living or working environment, does it give the impression of spaciousness or does it look and feel cluttered? Clutter, too much furniture or "stuff," inappropriately placed, can cause Chi to slow down and stagnate in your space. Your life will begin to reflect a corresponding "stuckness" the longer you stay in a cluttered environment.	Enter your *clutter* quotient in the gray box with 5 being quite orderly and 1 being very cluttered.
2. Natural Light	Is there sufficient natural light to give a sense of illumination and inviting warmth? This is especially important for entryways where adequate lighting creates a feeling of welcome. Or is your environment insufficiently lit or bathed in the glare of cold, harsh lighting, draining your Chi, resulting in decreased energy, creativity or productivity?	Enter your *natural light* quotient with 5 indicating good light and 1 indicating harsh, dim or insufficient light.
3. Peacefulness	Do you get a feeling of peacefulness when entering your space? Your environment should be a "cozy nest" where you can count on feeling safe and relaxed. If it is a work space, is it also a place where you can easily focus and be creative? Or does your environment feel disturbed, stressful or agitated?	Enter your *peacefulness* quotient with 5 indicating a good feeling of tranquility in your home and 1 indicating agitation or unrest.
4. Color Comfort	Are the colors in your environment attractive and consistent with your personal preferences? If you do not live with colors you love, it will be very difficult to ever feel completely at ease. If you prefer cool colors like blue and green, you'll never feel completely comfortable with warm shades like red and orange.	Enter your *color comfort* quotient with 5 indicating being surrounded by colors you love and 1 indicating incompatible colors (or no colors).
5. Things You Love	Do you surround yourself with items you love? There's an old saying, "Everything is talking to you all the time, make sure they have nice things to say." Living with things you no longer need, want, use or love depletes your Chi because they're alive with the negative memories and associations you give them.	Enter your *things you love* quotient with 5 indicating being surrounded with items you love and 1 indicating negative or no attachment to the items that surround you.
6. Command Position	Can you see the main entrance of the room from the bed, desk or anywhere you normally sit and relax without having to turn your head more than 45 degrees? Or are you positioned where you cannot clearly see the doorway, creating subconscious feelings of being on guard by not having a clear view of what might be "coming at you."	Enter your *command position* quotient with 5 indicating command positions in the places you frequent and 1 indicating no command positions.
7. Spreading your Wings	Does your environment help you feel nurtured, inspired and free to be you? Is your consciousness reflected in your reality? Or does your environment create feelings of restriction or limitation? Do you feel unsupported or uncomfortable, a stranger in your own environment?	Enter your *spreading your wings* quotient with 5 indicating no feelings of limitation related to environment and 1 indicating strong feelings of limitation.

© Copyright 2005, Sandi Miller. All Rights Reserved. No reproduction allowed without written consent from publisher.

8. Entryways	Does the entryway to your environment attract or repel? Is the path to your door inviting, attractive and well-marked or is it overgrown with plants, cluttered or poorly lit? Is your front door neat and attractively painted or varnished? When you enter your environment's "main mouth of Chi" does it open easily or only partway due to clutter behind it, symbolizing obstacles to the flow of abundance into your life?	Enter your *entryways* quotient with 5 indicating a clean, inviting entry and 1 indicating a choked, unattractive entryway.	
9. Sounds	Does your environment make sounds you love: the gentle ticking of a precious grandfather clock, the delicate rustling of leaves outside your window, soothing, trickling water, soft relaxing music? Or are your environmental sounds irritating, with noises like traffic, sirens, trains, noisy neighbors, or barking dogs?	Enter your *sounds* quotient with 5 indicating delightfully inviting sounds and 1 indicating irritating sounds that evoke negative emotions.	
10. Mirrors	Are your mirrors hung properly, creating a feeling of "opening up your space"? Do they activate energy and reflect beauty, doubling the effect of abundant, positive Chi in your environment? Or are they cracked, broken or improperly hung, reflecting chaos, disruption, or otherwise undesirable images? Improperly placed or chosen mirrors can lead to health concerns such as headaches, neck and shoulder pains, sinus problems or sleep disturbances.	Enter your *mirrors* quotient with 5 indicating reflections of beauty and abundance and 1 indicating reflections of negative environmental elements.	
11. Broken or Unhealthy Items	Do your appliances, clocks, furniture, and electrical equipment work properly or are they in need of repair? Are your plants healthy and thriving or do they look sickly? The energy of broken, useless or dying items in your environment will often manifest in your life as roadblocks, stagnant energy or missed opportunities.	Enter your *broken items* quotient with 5 indicating your environment is running smoothly and 1 indicating many items in disrepair or needing attention.	
12. Plumbing	Do all your plumbing fixtures work properly, creating a healthy flow of essential, fresh Chi in and out of your environment? Or does your shower faucet leak, toilet handle stick, or sprinkler system puddle up, symbolizing vital Chi being wasted or "going down the drain"? This will often show up in your life as a nagging feeling of money or other valuable resources slipping through your fingers.	Enter your *plumbing* quotient with 5 indicating no leaks anywhere and 1 indicating it's time to call a plumber!	

© Copyright 2005, Sandi Miller. All Rights Reserved. No reproduction allowed without written consent from publisher.

Instructions for scoring: Add the numbers in the far right column.

48-60 Indicates a high level of comfort and harmoniously flowing Chi. You, your family and your guests feel fortunate to be in this environment. *The Art of Living* will help you advance to the next level of creating a balanced, joyful environment.

31-47 Indicates you could benefit from incorporating skills and techniques from *The Art of Living* to create your dream environment, your "home for the soul."

12-30 Indicates that you probably are not very comfortable or happy in your environment and will benefit enormously by applying the easy, creative skills and techniques in *The Art of Living* to enhance your environment and change your life!

Section Two:
The Art of Mental Flow

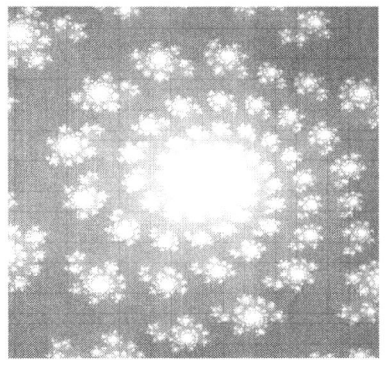

Creating Mental Flow with Inner Feng Shui

Understanding some of the fundamental yet potent applications of Feng Shui explored in the previous chapter may seem at first very much like "concentrated common sense." If you experienced any "aha" moments wondering, "Now, why didn't I think of that?" then you can be confident you are on a positive path toward discovering what works for you *personally* in creating your own unique environmental bliss.

Let's take that understanding a step farther. Logically, we know that if all that was required was to place our furniture in exactly the right position in order for our lives to be functioning perfectly, we would certainly have done that a *long* time ago and our hearts desires would already be manifesting in our lives. Harmonious environmental flow is essential, but it is only part of the formula for attracting and sustaining abundant health, wealth and happiness. We must also pay close attention to our attitudes, beliefs, thoughts and self-talk, our mental flow. Where attention goes, *intention* flows.

Just as stuck environmental energy hinders free flowing Chi on the physical level, stuck mental energy often shows up as preoccupation with future fears or past regrets. It prevents us from living "here and now," being present to our life in the moment our life is actually going on. In the past, present-moment life may have seemed too unhappy, uncertain or terrifying for us to be fully *present*, so we learned to live for a future when we hoped life would finally be safe and happy.

Though we survived those difficult years and the fears that once drove us to seek solace in our future fantasies are no longer a clear and present danger, we are still in the habit of survival mode thinking, which effectively keeps us from being aware of how life is occurring in the present moment. By becoming aware of old thought habits, beliefs, judgments, doubts or fears that no longer serve their original purpose, we can choose to adopt more relevant, self-supporting thoughts that allow us to awaken to our present-moment world, and thus begin creating a far more positive mental flow.

Becoming increasingly aware of our negative self-talk and mastering our ability to consciously choose more self-supportive, nurturing and uplifting thoughts is at the very heart of creating an experience of lasting happiness and abundance. When we begin freeing ourselves from the limitations of false or outmoded thoughts, habits and beliefs, and replacing them with positive, loving and nurturing thoughts, we naturally begin feeling more balanced and blessed.

In this chapter, we'll explore some of the ways that have been most beneficial in my personal quest for unblocking mental stuckness and maintaining harmonious mental, emotional and spiritual inner/Chi.

> *"Expect your every need to be met, expect the answer to every problem, expect abundance on every level, expect to grow spiritually."*
>
> - Eileen Caddy, *The Dawn of Change*

Self-nurturing

> *"Every day we wake with a certain amount of mental, emotional and physical energy that we spend throughout the day. If we allow our emotions to deplete our energy, we have no energy to change our life or to give to others."*
>
> - Don Miguel Ruiz, *The Four Agreements*

How many times have you heard, "First, you must learn to love *yourself* before you will really know how to love anyone else." For years, I didn't understand how the love I desired to receive from someone *else* was something I could give to myself. How could I give affection, nurturing, reassurance or satisfying companionship to *me*? Clearly, those were all things I believed I needed to receive from others, from outside of myself.

Slowly, over many years of dissatisfaction from the repeated disappointment of unmet expectations, I began to realize that maybe I was *never* going to find true happiness "out there." I began to accept that maybe happiness really was an "inside job."

> *"There is no way to happiness. Happiness is the way."*
>
> - Dr. Wayne Dyer, *The Power of Intention*

I began remembering activities I used to love that always seemed to lift me up, fill the void and make me feel better - activities like creative work with my hands, singing, dancing, taking baby-steps toward finishing my first book *even when I didn't feel like it*, reading uplifting material, taking a yoga class, listening to music I love or just completing something I've been meaning to get around to for far too long. I have found that even the smallest amount of sorting and clearing away clutter in my environment can create a positive shift in my attitude and is one more way I take care of me. It's kind of like the advice we hear just before take-off on an airplane, "Put your own oxygen mask on *first* before assisting others." Taking care of me *first* by investing time, energy and attention on my needs, gives me far greater ability to give to others.

> *"Paying attention to your needs, and living in a way that nourishes you is not self-indulgence, it's self-preservation!"*
>
> - Author unknown

Awareness

Challenging yourself to become more mindful, more aware in each moment, greatly enhances your experience of flow on all levels. In *The Game of Life*, Florence Scovel Shinn advises cultivating an attitude of awareness and expectancy, staying open to new ideas, intuitions, inspirations and answers coming to you *any* time from *any* source. You are truly living when you are awake to each moment because the present moment is all you ever really have.

> "The Present is a present."
>
> - Annie Dillard, *Pilgrim at Tinker Creek*

Often we find ourselves mentally and emotionally caught up in the drama of our day-to-day lives and completely lose sight of the *bigger* picture. We forget that each of us has a higher, nobler calling (our personal mission, purpose or dharma) than just trudging along day after difficult day, preoccupied with feeling stuck in far less than satisfying relationships or careers. As the dream of an abundant life for ourselves and our loved ones begins to dim, we lose sight of all the good that exists in our lives, everything we already have to be grateful for, and instead focus on all we don't yet have or all that seems wrong in our lives.

> *"Before, I always lived in anticipation... that it was all a preparation for something else, something 'greater,' more 'genuine.' But that feeling has dropped away from me completely. I live here-and-now, this minute, this day, to the full, and the life is worth living."*
>
> - Etty Hillesum

Carolyn Myss, Ph.D., author of *Anatomy of the Spirit*, suggests we begin cultivating mindfulness by mastering our response to life. When we respond with an automatic "knee-jerk" reaction, we are responding from our past experience, past pain, past emotions, past fears. However, when we master our response to life, when we choose to respond from loving acceptance of what is and be fully present, we will find our days taking on a rhythm of ease and grace.

> *"Only with awareness do you have the possibility of transforming your dream. If you have the awareness that the whole drama of your life is the result of what you believe, and what you believe is not real, then you can begin to change it."*
>
> - Don Miguel Ruiz, *The Four Agreements*

We will have access to far more options when we are not thrown off balance by allowing past programming to control our present moment responses. If we do not allow our past programming to be in control, we will be in a position to choose more positive and proactive attitudes which will help keep us in the *present* and not off in past pain or future worries. When we are more *present*, we will be receptive partners with our natural intuition, which directs us in knowing which opportunities and actions are appropriate in any given moment. We then become victorious creators of positive flow rather than powerless victims of habitual response.

> "The present moment is where life can be found, and if you don't arrive there, you miss your appointment with life."
>
> -Thich Nhat Hanh, *The Present Moment*

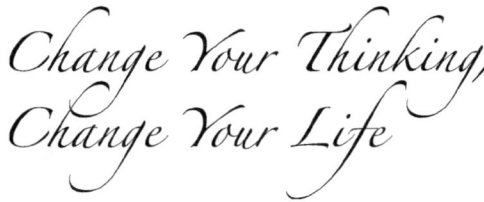

"When you change the way you look at things, the things you look at change."

- Dr. Wayne Dyer

"Change your thinking, change your life," means that when we are willing to change the way we think by monitoring our thoughts, beliefs, and responses to *any* situation, then we actually become creators of our own inner world as we *wish* it to be.

The universe acts much like a giant photocopier. It precisely replicates our thoughts over and over, as often as we think them. If our thoughts are negative or limiting, that is what the universe will repeatedly keep feeding back to us. The only way to stop this debilitating cycle is to change the thinking patterns that no longer serve us.

How? It's useful to remember that we didn't create our current belief system overnight. In fact many of our thoughts and beliefs aren't really *our* thoughts at all. We inherited them by innocently accepting the beliefs of those responsible for our upbringing. By becoming aware of and changing any negative self-talk messages we've unwittingly absorbed, and consciously adopting more positive, supportive beliefs, we begin reclaiming our personal power and creating a life that supports who we *really* are.

If it is true that our physical world is a projection of our personal beliefs and level of awareness, then it stands to reason that when we adopt more positive beliefs along with raising our level of awareness and becoming more present, the perception of our physical world will shift to reflect those positive beliefs. In his book *How to Get What You Really, Really, Really, Really Want*, Dr. Wayne Dyer says that the "good news is: we attract what we want by focusing on it. But the bad news is: that we will also attract anything we continually focus on *not* wanting!"

> "Thought > Feeling > Action > Results."
> - T. Harv Eker

In *The Game of Life*, Florence Scovel Shinn teaches us that our lives are a direct result of the thoughts we think and that everything in this manmade world came into being because someone first had a thought about it, then took the action necessary to manifest the thought into physical reality. The thoughts we hold in our consciousness create the reality we experience. Our *inner* experience is reflected in our *outer* reality.

> *"The invisible creates the visible."*
> - T. Harv Eker

Maybe you've heard someone say, "There's just not enough money, money doesn't grow on trees, money is scarce, money is never given freely." If we believe in scarcity or lack, that will be the belief the universe acts upon on our behalf. Few of us believe we are *choosing* to live without the things we want whether it's money, relationships, good health or happiness. But the truth is that our unconscious, negative belief systems are actually creating the *outcome* of our conscious reality.

> *"The creative Source reacts to your belief in shortages with a fulfillment of your belief."*
>
> - Dr. Wayne Dyer

If you consistently feel you are in a state of emotional chaos, you can bet that negative self-talk is also present. If you find yourself thinking fearful or self-limiting thoughts about a particular situation, ask yourself if this is how you really want the situation to be? If not, re-frame your self-talk to include more positive statements like, "My situation is now changing for the better," or "Good fortune is mine here and now," or "I am now attracting ideal relationships into my life," or "I attract only beauty." Your words have the power to create or destroy so be mindful to choose words with positive significance. Think positive thoughts. Say positive words. Learn how to speak the language of *positivity* by reframing negative self-talk and it will fundamentally assist you in turning your life around.

"Big success is not built on success. It is built on adversity, frustration, failure, sometimes even catastrophe, and the way we deal with it and turn it around."

- Sumner Redstone (owner of Viacom, CBS, Paramount Pictures and Blockbuster Video. Personal worth: nine billion)

How do we go about changing our thinking? Great question! Neale Donald Walsh suggests in *Conversations with God* that we must reverse the old adage "think before you act" and allow yourself to "*act* before you think." Our thoughts are trained to keep us in our past behaviors and if we choose to act spontaneously different, we can literally re-train our thinking, bypassing the old thought process until our mind understands and accepts the benefits of the change.

Let's say for example you have a personal "story" that you are shy, not good with people or don't make friends easily. Your way of being, until now, has been to keep to yourself and not risk rejection by attempting to get to know other people or make friends. One day, you notice someone at work wearing an attractive new suit and your first impulse is to enthusiastically say, "Wow, you look great today!" But, your mind quickly seizes control and confronts you with all the seemingly *good* reasons why it's a *bad* idea to pay them a compliment, or say anything at all to them. Your mind issues stern warnings like, "You don't know them very well, they may get the wrong idea and think you're flirting with them," or "They may not accept your compliment and then you will *really* feel stupid. You are better off not saying anything." Get the idea? TOO RISKY! At least, that's what your belief system, tells you.

Your mind can very quickly control your behavior and stop you from taking a simple action that otherwise might brighten not only the day of the person receiving the compliment but also your own. You will receive a *lift* from your spontaneous *gift*, that of feeling generous, expansive and magnanimous. Generous, expansive and magnanimous feels really great! Plus, you never can predict how your spontaneous gesture may positively affect many others. The person you complimented may be inspired to "pass it on" and the next person might do the same and so on. It's like a pebble tossed in a pond producing ripples that eventually touch every part of the shore. One very small gesture often has far-reaching effects.

"Behavior is not innate. People can learn to be positive."

- Dr. Robert Carr

It all comes down to changing root thoughts by acting as if your new way of thinking is already true. Changing your negative root thought will pay far greater dividends than almost anything else you do to create personal balance. Act quickly before your mind tries to quash the idea, before you realize you're taking new action. Take baby steps and make small gestures when you see the opportunity to behave in a way that supports the new beliefs you want to enforce and your mind will soon release negative patterns and replace them with new positive thoughts of your choosing. Your new positive thoughts will soon take root and bear fruit.

"Roots create the fruits"

- T. Harv Eker

Helpful Tips for Changing Root Thoughts

1. Take spontaneous, quick action, acting *as if* your new way of thinking is already true for you.

2. Make small gestures, baby steps that support your new beliefs.

3. Repeat steps one and two as needed!

   "Whether you believe you can or you can't, you are right!"

   – Henry Ford

Your Life is a Mirror

Your life is a mirror of what you *believe* you deserve. The law of the universe will not violate your own belief about what you *think* is true for you, nor will it provide you with anything you don't believe you *deserve* to receive, no matter how much you want it!

> *"You can choose to believe in anything. And that includes believing in yourself!"*
>
> - Don Miguel Ruiz, *The Four Agreements*

It is also true that if you believe you *cannot* have something, it produces the same result as not desiring to have it. Another way of saying this is if you *want* something, if you feel something is missing in your life, you are merely affirming that you don't *have* it. Yearning for something, no matter how much you want it, keeps it in the category of "lack" and blocks it from you.

> *"When we operate from scarcity, we attract poverty."*
>
> - Terry Cole Whitaker

It's similar to the principle of "If you love something, let it go. If it comes back to you, it is yours. If is does not, then it never really was." The challenge is in letting go of the *attachment to outcome* of any event turning out the way you want it to. Far easier said than done! When we wish or want things to be different than they are, the result is often upset or suffering because it takes us out of *present moment acceptance* and projects our attachment to a desired outcome. This is not to say we must let go of our desired goals and dreams. Rather, the more we release *needing* things to turn out as we'd like along with doing our best to accomplish our objectives in the *present moment*, the more we suffer less disappointment from having unmet expectations. It is the principle of high commitment (to our goals) and low attachment (to desired outcome) that is key here.

> *"Desire is derived from two roots meaning, 'to move toward your star.' So, desire, by definition, must include a belief in the possibility of that which you desire."*
>
> - Dennis McCarthy

Helpful tip: Practice saying out loud as if you really mean it: "I can do it," "I do____," "I am____," (fill in the blank with positive statements). "I can't, I don't, I never" are words of lack and limitation and will never attract abundance, so always try to use positive, present tense words in your affirmations.

Thoughts Made Manifest

In *Rich Dad, Poor Dad*, Robert Kiyosaki suggests that if you're the kind of person who is waiting for the *right* thing to happen, you might wait for a very long time. It would be as if you are waiting for all the traffic lights to be green for five miles before starting a trip. The truth is, few people realize that good fortune is a function of choice, not chance. Those who create their own good luck are able to take whatever happens to them and make it even better.

> "Great good fortune can only come to a person who is balanced and feels fortunate."
>
> - Stuart Wilde

If you don't feel fortunate or worthy of whatever you desire to bring into your life, it will be very difficult for you to attract and maintain it. Your beliefs about not being worthy of the life you desire can actually *block* your good fortune. That's why it is crucial to look at any beliefs you hold that may be blocking your ability to attract the abundance and happiness you so richly deserve.

Author Deepak Chopra teaches that our physical world, the world of our five senses, is a projection of our current level of awareness in our waking state of consciousness. It's as if what's going on *inside* of us becomes *reflected*, showing up as what goes on *outside* of us. He claims that synchronicity *increases* when we introduce "intent" into the conscious energy field. This connects us with cosmic mind. Our intention *reorients* the field. It's like the old saying, "Ask and you shall receive." If your intentions aren't clear to you, how would you recognize the synchronicities when they occur? You must know what your intentions are in order to recognize them and take appropriate action when opportunities show up.

> *"If you ask for success and prepare for failure, you get the situation you prepared for. You must prepare for what you want even though there's no sign of it yet. You must know your good fortune is on its way to you now."*
>
> - Florence Scovel Shinn

Fear = Mental Clutter

> "Fear itself does not exist in the world – there are only thoughts and avoidance behaviors."
>
> - Dr. Wayne Dyer

Recognizing and eliminating fearful thoughts is a major challenge in changing negative thinking and enhancing positive mental flow. Fear, or more accurately the *illusion* of fear, is simply a coagulation of mental energy. In other words, fear is "mental clutter."

> "We respond not to reality but to perception."
>
> - Phil McGraw, Ph.D.

After 20 years living and working in the beautiful Pacific Northwest United States, it became increasingly clear that I really needed to be living in the Los Angeles area, for personal as well as professional reasons. Yet, for a long time, I avoided making the move because of my perceived fears that I would be swallowed by an enormous earthquake, caught in the cross fire of gang violence or stuck in countless hours of notorious bumper-to-bumper freeway traffic. Those fears, that *mental clutter*, kept me from making a move to a place that ultimately turned out to be a great place for me to live and work.

> "Life isn't about what happens to us. It's about how we perceive what happens to us."
>
> - Buddha

Four years after mustering the courage to move to Southern California, I was living in the peaceful suburb of Simi Valley at the time of the massive Northridge quake, just three miles from the epicenter. Although it was a terrifying experience from which my house and much of its contents suffered extensive damage, my family and I survived intact with the knowledge and confidence that even massive earthquakes are totally survivable. In time, I conquered my fear of freeways by learning how to arrange my schedule to limit navigating roads during peak times. And, I discovered that not only are there relatively few southland areas ravaged by gang violence, but that there are many beautiful, friendly and safe locations to live in addition to great year-round weather. All in all, I found Southern California a very good fit, a discovery I would never have made had I let my fears control my choices.

> "Every time we face one of our fears, we are a little more free."
>
> - Don Miguel Ruiz, *The Four Agreements*

The trick is to *Feel the Fear and Do It Anyway* as Susan Jeffers' wonderful book teaches. When we choose to face our fears and risk a new way of being in the world, we create new opportunities for unlimited potential in our lives. By taking the necessary action to face and work through them, we begin freeing up coagulated mental energy that we previously did not have access to. The next time you face a fear, take a moment to notice if you experience an appreciable energy *rush* immediately following. It's a very freeing feeling. Fear *blocks* flow. Face your fears and watch flow grow! What fear is preventing you from taking a necessary risk today that might bring you one step closer to your heart's desire?

> *"Life is either a daring adventure, or it is nothing at all."*
>
> - Helen Keller

Dreams and Goals: Things to Try

Create a list of some of your most heartfelt dreams and goals. Next to each, jot down a couple of quick and easy action steps you could take right now that will begin moving you in the direction of your heart's desire. Things like making a phone call you've been putting off, writing a long overdue letter, doing some research you've been intending to do at the library or on the Internet, cleaning out a file or desk drawer you've thrown all your inspired notes into for a creative writing project, or maybe tending to a relationship that needs mending.

List Your Dreams and Goals

Fears and Concerns: Things to Try

Now, looking at those action steps you've just listed, create another list of fears and concerns that may be preventing you from taking the action necessary to accomplish your dreams. Beside each fear, list one doable baby step you could take *right now* resulting in moving you a little bit closer to fulfilling your goals. For example, maybe doing some journaling around the fear, or talking with a trusted friend or therapist would help free up your personal energy and unblock the flow. By taking action externally toward revealing and healing core fears, you will naturally free up stuck internal energy and find it much easier to take any subsequent action steps necessary to move in the direction of your goals.

List Your Fears and Concerns

*To laugh is to risk appearing a fool.
Two weep is to risk appearing sentimental.
To reach out for another is to risk involvement.
To expose your feelings is to risk revealing your true self.
To place your ideas, your dreams, before a crowd, is to risk rejection.*

*To love is to risk not being loved in return.
To live is to risk dying.
To hope is to risk disappointment.
To try is to risk failure.*

*But risks must be taken, because the greatest hazard in life is to risk nothing.
Those who risk nothing, do nothing,
have nothing, and become nothing.*

*They may avoid present suffering and sorrow, but they will not learn, feel, change, grow, love, or live.
Chained by their fear, they are slaves who have forfeited their freedom.*

Only a person who risks is free.

- Anonymous

Acting on Your Intentions

Changing negative thoughts to positive thoughts, clearing out mental clutter, choosing self-nurturing behaviors and practicing present moment awareness are all essential for influencing the direction of your destiny.

Success doesn't just *happen* to people. It is the result of powerfully choosing thoughts, behaviors and actions conducive to success. You may be thinking, "Well, of course I *choose* success. Who wouldn't?" However, just saying you choose something and not backing it up by taking the necessary action steps, is equivalent to *not* choosing it at all. In fact, it may even be worse than deliberately *not* choosing. Because when you declare *not* to choose something and then take no corresponding action, you are at least being honest with yourself. You are actually acting with integrity for how you say you are choosing to live your life. If, however, you claim you do choose success but take no actions to support that choice, your word is hollow, creating conflicting intentions and internal imbalance.

I've heard it said that the shortest distance between two points is an intention. But intention is just the first step. We must back up our intentions with action. As the Japanese philosopher Takuan Soho said, "One may explain water, but the mouth will not become wet. Just understanding how deliciously refreshing a cool glass of water can taste will not quench our thirst. We must integrate our intention with the necessary action to obtain the glass of water and bring it to our parched lips and into our lives."

> "When you cannot make up your mind as to which course of action to take, choose the bolder!"
>
> - Author unknown

For example, if you choose to have good health, you must take actions that nurture the desired results: eat right and exercise. If you choose to have a great marriage or relationship, you must choose the actions that nurture and create that happy result. The same is true for anything else your heart desires.

> "Everything depends upon execution; having just a vision is no solution."
>
> - Stephen Sondheim

Life is not pre-destined. As long as we are breathing, we always have choice. Even if it seems like you have no choice, like everything is happening *to* you, you can still choose your *response* to every situation.

Action: Three Things to Try

Look at the list of action steps from the "Dreams & Goals" section. Decide on three that you would consider a top priority in improving the flow in your life and then work them into your current schedule. Using this process, you will experience daily momentum in the direction of your dreams.

List Your Action Steps

....

....

....

....

....

....

....

> "A body in motion tends to remain in motion, while a body at rest tends to stay at rest."
>
> - Isaac Newton

Keeping Promises, Creating Success

> "Judge your success by what you had to give up in order to get it! Great love and great achievements involve great risk."
>
> - Author unknown

How do you make a choice or commitment that you *know* you can keep? Let's take for example, New Year's resolutions. Why are they so hard to stick to? In the first place, New Years resolutions are really a deception. The problem is that we try to keep these resolutions by exerting our *will power*. Will power is basically an emotion, and emotions are fickle. So will power can't be counted on and the bottom line is, will power just doesn't work! Anyone who's ever relied on will power trying to stay on diet after diet to lose weight knows this is true.

> "Environment is stronger than will power."
>
> - Yogananda

The good news is you don't need a resolution to make a promise that will stick. What you need is a program that will guide and carry you through to completion once the emotional excitement of your commitment is gone. It's easy to keep your commitment in the beginning when you are all pumped up, but what do you do a few weeks later when you're no longer excited and frankly just don't *feel* like it anymore? That's when you need a strategy! And according to author and television talk show host Dr. Phil McGraw, it needs to have several elements:

1. Be specific. Say exactly what it is you want. Dr. Phil advises us to "name it to claim it." If you want to lose a certain amount of weight - be *specific*. Is it 10, 20, 30 or 100 pounds?

2. Be realistic. Don't set unrealistic goals for yourself. For example, don't try to lose 100 pounds in 30 days. You will be setting yourself up for failure.

3. Have accountability. If we don't have some way of "holding our feet to the fire," we will cheat! Enlist someone you can count on: your mate, a parent or a good friend, someone you actually report to once a week on whether you did what you said you would do or not.

4. Have a time line. Commit to a date "by when" you will accomplish your realistic goal. For example, "I will lose 20 pounds by_____." Or "I will heal the relationship with my mother-in-law by_____." You *must* have a time line. Otherwise your goal is just a dream. In fact, the time line makes all the difference between a goal and a dream.

> "Goals are just dreams with a timeline and accountability."
>
> - Phil McGraw, Ph.D.

Taking one baby step at a time closes the gap between possibility (imagination) and fact (reality). Everybody has a "dream" of how they want their life to be, but unless you implement steps like the previous four mentioned that are specific and realistic, your goals will recede into the land of dreams and, like any other dream, will disappear every morning when you open your eyes.

> "Successful people do what unsuccessful people aren't willing to do."
>
> - Phil McGraw, Ph.D.

Self-discipline is an essential element of creating your own good fortune. When we mature, we learn that if we don't take charge and become accountable for creating the direction and flow of our own lives, *no one else will!*

Question: "Which demands more intelligence or presents the greater challenge: changing our environment to accommodate our needs or changing ourselves to adapt to our environment?"

Answer: "Changing our environment demands far more intelligence than changing ourselves. However, intelligence is of little value in the latter. That's why I believe that changing ourselves is a greater challenge: there's plenty of intelligence in the world, but the courage to do things differently is in short supply."

- Marilyn Vos Savant

Response-Ability

There is a story told of a young mother who heard the family cat screech in pain. Immediately, she suspected her son, Tommy, and went to find him. "Tommy, stop pulling the cat's tail," she scolded. "I'm not pulling his tail," Tommy replied. "I'm just standing on it. He is doing the pulling!"

Sound familiar? Tommy is simply behaving as he has been *taught* to behave by observing those around him regularly making a choice to blame someone (or something) else for their situation. When we place blame for circumstances in our lives and the lives of others on external factors such as the weather, the government, our parents, or as Tommy did with the cat, we are, in effect, relinquishing our personal freedom and responsibility. We are saying *they* are responsible for our woes or the situation. We give away our personal power when we say they are the reason things are the way they are or ignore our responsibility for what is occurring. We reclaim our power when we understand that they have no power over us except the power *we* give them or acknowledge our participation in creating what has occurred.

> "Unconscious people are always blamers."
>
> - Terry Cole Whitaker

"If our feelings control our actions it is because we have abdicated our responsibility and empowered them to do so. Reactive people are driven by feelings. Proactive people subordinate feelings to values."

- Stephen Covey, *The Seven Habits of Highly Effective People*

It is only when we understand our personal response-ability that we begin seeking solutions to our problems instead of looking for targets to blame our problems on. Becoming response-able by taking complete responsibility for ourselves and our choices is an indispensable step toward building a happier life, a life that not only makes a real difference for ourselves but for everyone around us.

Taking responsibility for yourself is easier than you might think. One clue that will always help you know when you are not accepting responsibility is when you notice yourself looking somewhere outside of yourself to place blame. Pointing the finger of response-ability away from you by blaming, keeps you from taking action to rectify the situation and being response-able for yourself.

"Our job is to master our response to our own life."

- Carolyn Myss, *The Anatomy of Spirit*

During the course of your lifetime, you will experience all sorts of things happening to you, for you and with you that you could never have imagined or seen coming. Your challenge will be to master your response to those experiences. How do you respond to situations that are seemingly out of your control? Many people, when faced with one of life's roadblocks, get stopped dead in their tracks feeling stuck and hopeless. "Why me?" they cry. "I'm a good person, why me?" Others might try the "ostrich strategy" immediately burying their head in the sand whenever faced with confrontation or challenge. Then there are the entrepreneurs, the pathfinders; some might dub them the "heroes." They look at the roadblock or obstacle and say, "What are my options here? It looks like I can go around it, climb it, honor it, blow it up, or do whatever I need to do to accomplish my goal and then... *move on!*" This last group has mastered their response to life's curve balls. They take action *no matter what* and the result is increased personal confidence and self-empowerment.

> *"Obstacles become opportunities"*
>
> - W. Mitchell, Author and Motivational Speaker

Responding to events is quite different from reacting to them. Our job is to not get lost in over-analyzing and speculating what we might have done to attract or cause negative situations into our life. Rather, our challenge is to upgrade our response to whatever life hands us. One excellent way to do this is by re-framing issues as blessings and choosing to see the gift in every occurrence.

> "It is not what happens to you, it is what you do about it."
>
> - W. Mitchell

It is important to realize that utilizing these powerful tools will not guarantee you will never again be triggered or respond in a less effective manner than you would like. It may be unrealistic to think you will reach the point of always responding precisely as you wish because as long as you are alive, you will be challenged with new personal development, growth and change. There is always the next challenge in your growth process that requires you to assimilate and adjust. A person living from conscious intention learns to adapt and accept the process of continually re-inventing themselves.

> "The moment you take responsibility for your life is the moment you're in charge of your life."
>
> - W. Mitchell

A good way to determine how much you've grown mentally, emotionally and spiritually is to reflect upon how you handled situations a year or two ago as opposed to how you handle the same or similar situations today. This observation is an excellent barometer of your inner growth progress and is usually quite validating. Our challenge is not to reach the point of never again having our triggers activated. Rather, it is to catch ourselves as quickly as possible when our triggers throw us off balance and implement positive course corrections.

> *"There is no such thing as a straight line to success. Correct and continue, correct and continue, correct and continue!"*
>
> - T. Harv Eker

How long do you hold onto an upset? How quickly you are able to effectively resolve and release issues of upset determines to a large degree the quality of your life. By choosing to stop "burning daylight" and more readily free yourself to be present, *right here and right now*, you are choosing to enhance whatever precious time you have. Notice how much time you are willing to invest in anger, fear, resentment, or any other negative state. The less time spent holding onto upset is another excellent measure of inner growth and transformation.

> *"In choosing our responses to circumstances, we powerfully affect our circumstances."*
>
> - Stephen Covey

Judgment: The High Cost of Needing to be Right

A mighty river starts with a meandering stream that began as a trickling creek and was once a single, tiny drop of water. In life, a world full of hate and fear begins with a single angry or negative thought, word or deed. Judgment is a potent act and when we judge someone else as bad or wrong, we are acting as if we think we have the *right* to judge. *Judging never makes us right*, it only makes it more difficult for us to see all sides of the picture. Based on fear, judgment separates us and creates a defensiveness that we have to maintain to prove how *right* we are now that we have judged another as wrong. Judgment alienates us from our hearts and from compassionate understanding.

There is a popular saying regarding conflict in relationships, "Do you want to be right, or do you want to be happy?" Or maybe you feel like the person who remarked, "I want to be right because that's what really makes me happy!" Relationships are always a two-way street and thinking we are right creates the illusion of safety. We mistakenly think that if we can convince ourselves we are right, we will be protected from the possibility of seeing our deepest fear manifest, for example that we may really be unlovable or unworthy, however illusory that fear may be.

Judgment is based on fear.

"Whenever you judge another human being, you do not define them with your judgment. You define yourself as someone who needs to judge."

- Dr. Wayne Dyer

Whenever we judge, the result is always alienation and separation. As we let go of judgment, we realize that even though we may disagree with someone's words or deeds, people truly do the best they know how to do in any given moment, and we begin to experience a freedom that can only be enjoyed by letting go of the need to judge. Poet Maya Angelou compassionately hits the bulls-eye with her theory that "when we know better, we do better."

Non-Judgment: Things to Try

What are some ways you can practice non-judgment in your life today? Try reminding yourself how important your friends and family are to you rather than becoming annoyed with their unique habits. How about a little more patience if you find yourself in a long checkout line at the supermarket or another driver cuts you off on the freeway? Or maybe practice refraining from negative comments on your teenager's unusual fashion sense. What are some ways you can practice not needing to be right? List them on the following page.

List Ways You Can Practice Non-Judgment

The Healing Power of Self-Forgiveness

"There is no revenge so complete as forgiveness."

- Josh Billings (1815-1885) Humorist and Lecturer

Why should we forgive *ourselves*? We aren't the cause of our own anger or pain. Or, *are* we? Remember, we are always response-able and it is our choice how we react moment by moment, even though it may not seem like it at the time. Even not choosing is a choice!

For example, imagine your best friend of twenty years saying something that seems incredibly thoughtless to you at the time. Seemingly unaware that your feelings have been hurt, they go about their business but you are left fuming, not knowing what to say or do to resolve the issue. So, in frustration, you choose to do *nothing*. As time goes by, your anger and resentment builds, creating a sense of separation between two old and dear friends.

"Resentment is just another way of hanging on! As long as I hold onto it, I hold onto you!"

- Author unknown

When you choose to really *feel* your feelings, you can then identify the judgment you've made about your friend. Maybe it was something like, "A really good friend wouldn't have said something like that." Or, maybe more to the point, "They are so wrong for saying that," or "How dare they?"

Once you've identified your judgment of them, notice how this judgment acts as a mirror for one of your own insecurities or fears. Maybe you got the message when you were little that nothing you ever said or did was *good enough,* and on some level, you still hold the illusion that you may not be good enough to deserve the love and respect you desire. Maybe down deep you're really afraid you aren't worthy of that level of caring. In an effort to protect your own fragile self-image (ego) you project your erroneous illusion or belief of unworthiness onto others when you feel wronged by them. Whenever we feel emotionally triggered, it's a pretty safe bet that we are projecting our own fears and insecurities onto others. If you judge your old pal as not being a truly good friend, you may have a core belief that says, "I don't deserve better," or "If I was really lovable, my friend wouldn't have said or done that." As you can see, the first place to start the forgiveness process begins with our own faulty beliefs.

> "You've got to 'feel it to heal it'."
>
> - Phil McGraw, Ph.D.

The self-forgiveness process is really quite easy. We simply forgive ourselves for *judging ourselves* as not being deserving, worthy, good enough, or_____ (fill in the blank.) Once we forgive ourselves for the illusion we have accepted and believed up until now, the illusion begins to fade and lose its hold on us. We can then go to the next step and forgive ourselves for judging our friend as being thoughtless or _____ (fill in the blank). They may have indeed behaved thoughtlessly, but it is our judgment of them, and reaction *to* our judgment, that is actually the central culprit of our upset.

Our reaction to our judgment keeps us in a state of emotional imbalance as we *fight to be right* and makes it nearly impossible for us to respond in a manner that will bring peace, healing and completion rather than prolonging the pain. By accepting response-ability for our actions and reactions, and forgiving our judgment of others, as well as ourselves, we are well on our way to reclaiming our authentic power.

> "Holding onto anger and resentment is like drinking poison and expecting someone else to die!"
>
> - Author unknown

Once self-forgiveness has been implemented, you will notice a shift that often feels like a load has been lifted from you, a wonderful sense of freedom and lightness. A feeling that you are now free to choose how you want your life to be. Your actions and choices will no longer be coming from your triggered emotions, but rather from your heart.

> *"Once you forgive yourself, the self-rejection in your mind is over. Self-acceptance begins, and the self-love will grow so strong that you will finally accept yourself just the way you are. That's the beginning of the free human. Forgiveness is the key. You will know you have forgiven someone when you see them or hear their name and you no longer have an emotional reaction."*
>
> - Don Miguel Ruiz, *The Four Agreements*

Self-forgiveness is an essential key to inner freedom. Once we experience the healing power of this infinitely effective life skill, we need never feel victimized again. Implementing regular self-forgiveness is an essential step toward mastering our own destiny. No longer will we find ourselves controlled by endless every day mini-traumas/dramas. We will finally be in the position of choosing our response to *everything* that comes our way, and *that* is true power!

> *"I am what I am, and what I am is wonderful."*
>
> - Sarah Ban Breathnach, *The Simple Abundance Companion*

Forgiveness: Things to Try

1. Identify an upset, past or present, and allow yourself to fully experience your feelings around it (i.e. anger, sadness, jealousy, hurt, embarrassment, etc).

   ....

   ....

   ....

   ....

   ....

2. Identify the judgment(s) *behind* the feeling. For example, she/he did or said something I feel upset by, therefore I am judging them as thoughtless/wrong/mean/inconsiderate, etc.

   ....

   ....

   ....

   ....

   ....

3. Lovingly and compassionately, apply self-forgiveness to the hurt and judgment. For example, begin by forgiving yourself for judging *them*: "I forgive myself for judging _____ (fill in their name) as thoughtless, mean or _____" (describe your feelings). I find it helpful to add: "And the truth is, I know they are doing the very best they possibly can at this time."

....

....

....

....

....

....

....

....

....

....

....

....

....

....

4. Now, the final and most important step: "Self" forgiveness. Lovingly and compassionately forgive your *Self*. For example "I forgive myself, for judging myself, as not being deserving of respect, love, kindness or_____ from_____" (insert their name). And, again, I like to add: "And the truth is, I am doing the very best I know how to do at this time in my life. As I know better, I'll do better."

....

....

....

....

....

....

....

....

"You can search the whole world over and never find anyone as deserving of your love as yourself."

- Buddha

The Power of Gratitude

"If the only prayer you ever say your entire life is Thank You, it will be enough."

- Meister Eckhart, *The Power of Now*

In *Simple Abundance*, Sarah Ban Breathnach writes that the more you recognize that which you already have in your life to be grateful about, you begin to see even *more* to be grateful for. She suggests keeping a "gratitude journal" by taking a few moments at the end of each day to write down several things you feel particularly grateful for. This small but powerful act shifts your attention to a higher level by placing awareness on all the good already existing in your life. It helps foster an "attitude of gratitude" and abundance.

Becoming aware of everything you already have to be grateful for and acknowledging your gratitude on a regular basis is an excellent way of increasing abundance in your life. Instead of focusing on what is *lacking* in your world by thinking thoughts like: "If only I made more money, had a newer car, better health or a more thoughtful mate, *then* I would be happy." Focus instead on acknowledging just how *wealthy* you already are. Do you have a roof over your head? Do you have a job, or better still, a job you like?

Are you and your loved ones healthy? *Feeling* grateful and *expressing* that gratitude for day-to-day things you may often take for granted, shifts the focus from what you perceive is *missing* in your world and moves your attitude into a state of grateful acceptance for how wealthy you already are.

> *"Good the more communicated... grows!"*
>
> - John Milton, English Poet

Author Joan Borysenko believes that the old saying, "what you give, you also receive" is actually an inviolable law. Expressing your gratitude may seem like such a simple thing, but the effect is gigantic because it results in creating more love in the world.

> *"When your heart is filled with gratitude, when you can just go out and feel how lucky you are that the world is there for you, and how lucky you are that there are people out there trying to enrich your world, it's a lot easier to be loving—to yourself and to others."*
>
> - Rabbi Harold Kushner

Radio personality David Brudnoy has described his professional demeanor as egocentric, spoiled, arrogant and controlling prior to his brush with a near fatal illness. As he emerged from a coma and began his long road to recovery, he was deluged with tens of thousands of cards from loyal listeners urging him not to give up. "Those sentiments changed my life," Brudnoy said. "I realized I needed other people to survive. I became less demanding. Now, if someone is late, I don't care. I'm much easier to be around." In his book *Life Is Not a Rehearsal*, he chronicles his recovery, and to this day, monitors his thoughts so his old thinking patterns don't return. He adds, "Every time I get cocky and start having a thinking relapse, it seems I get a physical reversal. I feel weak. I'm being reminded of something: I could go at any time. So while I'm here, I've got to appreciate everything - friends, my job, the freshness of the day."

When was the last time you noticed the fresh scent of the breeze as it caressed your cheek or felt gratitude for the songbird's sweet song or appreciated the simple beauty and elegance of nature? Remembering to notice and appreciate the little everyday blessings in your world is a powerful practice for nurturing and increasing the experience of gratitude in your life.

> *"We are all given so much, and don't notice. I want to feel gratitude because gratitude is realistic, realism reflects truth, and truth is liberating. So to say I want to be more grateful is, I guess, to say I want to be freer."*
>
> - Peggy Noonan

Gratitude: Things to Try

Strengthen your "attitude of gratitude" muscle once a day by finding at least one *new* thing to appreciate, something you've never acknowledged gratitude for before. The early morning mist on a field at dawn, the adoration in a loved ones eyes or even just hitting every green light on your way to work. It can be challenging trying to discover something you may never have noticed before or maybe *have* noticed but never acknowledged gratitude for. The result of this simple little exercise is that as you stretch yourself to pay attention during your day to finding one new gratitude item, you become increasingly aware of the abundance that already surrounds you... *all* the time! List something new you are grateful for:

....

....

....

....

....

....

Creating Lasting Change: Attitude Tips for Tough Times

When you find yourself in a rough patch and feeling as if you are "swimming against the current," seeking inspiration in people, places or books that inspire and nurture can be tremendously healing. We all need inspiration from time to time and we need each other most when we are experiencing periods of "dark nights of the soul."

> "That which is within you and expressed will set you free. That which is within you and not expressed will eat you from the inside."
>
> - The Gospel of Thomas

When we commit to having our life work the way we want it to, we are committing to a life that works at a higher level. Then, everything *not* at the higher level comes to the surface, and may feel quite uncomfortable or unsettling. You may notice an increase in negative thoughts designed to limit and keep you stuck in your current experience of life. Thoughts like, "Who am I to think I can actually achieve the success I desire?" or "I don't know if I really deserve positive change?" You might notice an increase in feelings of moodiness or emotional sensitivity as repressed fear of change comes up when you decide if the time has come to deal with (and heal) those fears once and for all.

> *"The fear of change, of relinquishing what we've always known and done and been, is what holds us back from our metamorphosis into a healthier, higher, more truly loving self."*
>
> – Robin Norwood, *Women Who Love Too Much*

It is helpful to remember that your emotions are tied to whatever your mind decides. So when you change your mind, sooner or later, your emotions will change as well. Try to be patient with yourself. Emotions often take time to incorporate change. Like a gigantic ocean liner that can take several miles to do a course correction from the tremendous momentum it has built up going in one direction, the same is true of our emotions. They *take the time they take* to course correct because of the momentum built up from a lifetime of prior mental agreements, beliefs and opinions. Be patient and kind with yourself and remember that you are doing very important work here. When we are in a hurry to get through a troubling issue, upsetting experience, or just to get something over with so we can get on with life, author Gunilla Norris says that what we are actually doing is "being in a hurry to *get our life over with,*" often carelessly disposing of our time in "units of meaninglessness, rather than units of meaning."

> *"As you get older, it gets simpler.*
> *When my feet are happy, I'm happy."*
>
> - Terry Cole Whitaker

For many of us, it seems that challenging experiences are often essential for our growth. The universe offers continual opportunities, sometimes one right after another, to help us deal with, move through and heal old wounds, fears, angers and resentments in order to absorb the lessons we most need to learn. When bad things happen to us, there is often the temptation to feel sorry for ourselves and ask, "Why me?" But there is little power in that question. True power comes by training ourselves to seek the opportunity for growth available in the experience itself. There is popular belief that there are *no accidents*. I've found that there is a reason for everything that happens even if it is not apparent at the time. I consider it my job to find the *gold* in each lesson.

> "Changes that are loved into being are permanent. Changes where you beat yourself up to accomplish them, are never permanent and will always go away."
>
> - Dr. Christiane Northrop,
>   Women's Bodies, Women's Wisdom

Change begins with a decision to take action. Conscious evolution is a continual process motivated by our desire to grow. Human beings are typically resistant to change and often wait until our circumstances force us to think, "This is it! I can't go on like this for another minute. Things must change!" It is often then that we sincerely desire to make change. However, if we really want to create positive change in our lives, we must learn not to look *outside* ourselves for that change to occur. Real and lasting change is an *inside* job.

To the degree that you choose to change, you are likely to experience a proportional degree of mental and emotional resistance as long-held limiting beliefs surface and fight for survival. Change is often perceived as a threat to those long held core beliefs. When fear comes up in response to change and you choose to revert to familiar behavior patterns of denial or avoidance, the disappointing result is almost always failure to reach your goals and a life lived beneath your full potential. Old habits and patterns will continue producing the same results they always have until you take a stand and choose more constructive ways of being.

> *"If what you've been looking for was where you've been looking, chances are you would have found it by now!"*
>
> - T. Harv Eker

Keeping Momentum: Things to Try

What are some obstacles you're facing right now? What are your greatest concerns about these obstacles? Consider your life if you broke through the barriers and moved beyond the obstacles into success. Consider your life if you accepted the situation as it is now. Which do you choose?

List Current Obstacles and Concerns

....

....

....

....

....

....

....

....

"The significant problems we face cannot be solved at the same level of thinking we were at when we created them."

- Stephen Covey

When you choose to create change, it's not unusual to experience some degree of physical resistance as well. It may be minimal physical discomfort: a headache or sore back muscles. Or it might be as debilitating as an illness that really knocks you for a loop. Physical sensations are often just temporary indications of old patterns surfacing to make way for the new change. Many times, things seem "darkest before the dawn" and what looks like discomfort or chaos can be reframed as a *good* thing and viewed as the freeing up of old, stuck, mental and emotional energy. You can choose to see these times as opportunities for inner housework that will clear the space for attracting positive outcomes. They are an indication that you are doing some very deep and extremely beneficial inner work!

Please be patient. Change doesn't happen overnight. When you notice yourself responding in familiar, less-than-positive ways, gently remind yourself that you've made a new choice in your life. This is where personally meaningful affirmations are excellent tools. They do not need to be elaborate or lengthy. They can be very simple, sometimes just one word or one phrase that reminds you of your choice to create positive change. An example of a simple yet powerful affirmation is: "I am now being the change I wish to see."

"Over, under, around or through, whatever it takes, I'll do."

- T. Harv. Eker

Obstacles are a sign of progress. Consider the Eker quote above and your list of obstacles from the previous page and list a few creative ways to go over, under, around or through your obstacles.

Summary of Mental Flow Tips

1. Practice moment-to-moment awareness. Find a way of meditating daily that appeals to you. Harness the power of your mind by learning to focus your thoughts and choose those that work *for* you, not against you.

2. Invest in yourself first and take care of your own needs so you can be of service to others.

3. Monitor your attitudes and beliefs. Eliminate "lack" consciousness and replace it with a positive, grateful attitude of expectancy.

4. Create a list of affirmations that are personally meaningful for you. Anytime you are feeling especially vulnerable, fearful or upset, choose affirmations from your list that give you positive mental fuel and break the cycle of negative, limiting thinking.

5. "Act before you think." Do something to brighten someone else's day before your mental chatter has the chance to talk your Self out of it. Give a sincere compliment or acknowledgment and watch how great it makes you both feel!

6. Take a good look at your fears and see them for the illusion they really are. Practice feeling your fear and taking consistent action anyway. Try to take at least one baby step everyday in the direction of your dreams.

7. Set realistic goals with timelines and accountability. Keep your promises, especially to yourself! The price of breaking agreements with yourself is loss of self trust, self-esteem and energy resulting in confusion and guilt. Remember, you get what you settle for.

8. Accept personal response-ability and be vigilant about upgrading your reaction to whatever life hands you. Learn how to master responding proactively.

9. Look for the "gold" in each lesson. Remember that the sun is always shining behind the clouds.

10. Choose whether you want to be right or whether you want to be happy. Notice when you are judging another as wrong and strive to create "win-win" results.

11. Notice when you are projecting one of your own self-limiting beliefs onto another (i.e. unworthiness). Whenever we find ourselves triggered, it is a pretty safe bet that the issue is with our *selves* and not another. Practice the fine art of self-forgiveness whenever you find yourself judging anyone else.

12. Practice an "attitude of gratitude" daily. Acknowledging and feeling good about the abundance you already have acts like a magnet to attract even more good fortune to you.

13. Create a network of support to help you through tough times. Don't put all your "eggs in one basket" and invest in only one or two primary relationships. Seek out others with similar interests and find fun ways to continually expand your social network. Churches, volunteer organizations, colleges, clubs, classes, anything where you have the opportunity to create the feeling of connectedness and belonging.

> *"In every field of human endeavor, all of the significant 'breakthroughs' were 'break-withs'...breaking with old ways of thinking."*
>
> - Stephen Covey

By integrating these simple yet highly effective attitude adjustments into your life, you will dramatically enhance your inner/Chi and attract more harmonious mental flow and synchronicity. On the pages that follow, you will find a thought-provoking attitude survey to help you chart inner areas most in need of your attention and intention.

The Art of Living Attitude Survey

1. Self Nurturing	In any given week, to what extent do you take care of *you*? How often do you reserve special *quality* time to do the things you love, unrelated to work, others, or obligation, purely for the sake of enjoyment?	Enter your *self-nurturing* quotient in the gray box with 5 indicating frequent self nurturing and 1 indicating rarely taking time for yourself.	
2. Awareness	To what extent are you consciously aware of what's happening inside and around you? Are you awake in your life or are you "sleepwalking" through it, focused more on the past or future than the present moment?	Enter your *awareness* quotient with 5 indicating you are often fully engaged in your life and 1 indicating that you are frequently "somewhere else."	
3. Monitoring your Thoughts	Do you choose your thoughts and reactions or do they seem to choose you? Do you monitor your thoughts and feelings as they occur?	Enter your *thought monitoring* quotient with 5 indicating frequent ability to choose your thought patterns and 1 indicating limited control of your mental and emotional reactions.	
4. Positive Thinking	Are you aware of how often you think positive vs. negative thoughts? Your thoughts become your reality. Do you frequently think self-defeating "I can't" thoughts or does your mind support you with uplifting "I can" thoughts?	Enter your *positive thinking* quotient with 5 indicating having very positive, confident thoughts and 1 indicating mostly negative thoughts.	
5. Heeding your Intuition	To what extent do you take action in response to your intuitive feelings or hunches? Or, do you dismiss "gut feelings" as unimportant or the product of an overactive imagination?	Enter your *honoring your intuition* quotient with 5 indicating frequent awareness of and action taken in response to intuitive feelings and 1 indicating seldom acting on hunches or feelings.	
6. Judgment	How often do you find yourself making judgments of others or yourself? Do you catch yourself making declarative statements either out loud or mentally about others or yourself, i.e., "He shouldn't have…" or "I should have…" or "If only…"?	Enter your *judgment* quotient with 5 indicating frequent judgment of self and others and 1 indicating acceptance of matters as they are, regardless of whether or not you are in agreement.	

© Copyright 2005, Sandi Miller. All Rights Reserved. No reproduction allowed without written consent from publisher.

7. Fear	Are you often fearful of relationships, finances, career, your health or that of your loved ones, your future or your past? Do your fearful thoughts create "stuckness" and immobility in your life progress?	Enter your *fear* quotient with 5 indicating seldom being stopped by fear and 1 indicating frequent fear and immobility.	
8. Responsibility	Do you take responsibility for your current situation or circumstances as opposed to blaming people or things outside of yourself?	Enter your *responsibility* quotient with 5 indicating a high degree of self-responsibility and 1 indicating frequent "blaming."	
9. Intentionality	Are you conscious of the intention behind your actions? Do you commit to a path that will lead where you want to go based on the intention you set and choose to bring into manifestation?	Enter your *intentionality* quotient with 5 indicating frequent attention to intention and 1 indicating very little awareness of intention.	
10. Healthy Boundaries	Are you skilled at establishing healthy boundaries that support your personal needs? Or do you find it difficult to "just say no" to others even when you *know* you want to? Do you often put others needs and desires ahead of your own regardless of the cost to your spirit?	Enter your *healthy boundaries* quotient with 5 indicating ease in setting self-nurturing boundaries and 1 indicating frequent difficulty with taking care of your own needs first.	
11. Just Do It!	Do you follow through with your plans based on your intentions all the way to completion? Or do you allow yourself to "slide" when it comes to accountability and commitment?	Enter your *doing it* quotient with 5 indicating excellence with following through and 1 indicating "all talk, no action."	

© Copyright 2005, Sandi Miller. All Rights Reserved. No reproduction allowed without written consent from publisher.

Instructions for scoring: Add the numbers in the far right column.

40-55 Indicates a high degree of comfort and positive mental energy. You are probably on the right path and generally happy. ***The Art of Living*** will help you balance your positive mental energy by helping you establish a healthy environment and looking at how spirit contributes to your overall wellbeing.

30-40 Indicates you could incorporate skills and techniques from ***The Art of Living*** to promote positive mental energy that will help you feel more in the flow of things.

10-30 Indicates that you are probably questioning your own personal tranquility, centeredness and balance. Try incorporating ideas for clearing mental clutter in the mental energy chapter in ***The Art of Living***. You'll find that being in the flow will lead to immediate positive changes in your life!

In Summary

As you know by now, *The Art of Living* is not just about changing environmental or outer circumstances. It is also about choosing another way of thinking, feeling and acting; a more effective and successful way than we have been accustomed to. Moment by moment, as we apply these principles, the circumstances of our lives begin to alter and shift; "miracles" begin occurring seemingly with little or no effort as change begins happening from the inside out.

The truth is, everyone wants to be happy, healthy, enjoy satisfying relationships, meaningful work and abundant financial security. Additionally, I believe we would all like to think we are making a contribution to the betterment of our planet. In order to achieve these goals, we need principles and values to live by - a philosophy that helps us understand our world and our relationship to it. There is no better time than now to release old, limiting thoughts and faulty beliefs and replace them with positive, prosperous and life-enhancing ideas, principles and values.

> *"A PRINCIPLE is a natural law. A PRACTICE is the expression of that natural law in a particular circumstance."*
>
> *- Stephen Covey*

In conclusion, if this material speaks to you in such a way that it sounds like "concentrated common sense," if it brings forth a response of "intuitive recognition," then you can be confident these words hold truth and opportunity for personal growth. Your degree of growth will be determined by your level of participation. The only way this material can fail to create magnificent shifts and even "miracles" in your life, is if you choose not to apply it.

Growing up with a dysfunctional/abusive stepparent, enduring a mentally and emotionally abusive marriage of my own as well as experiencing my share of personal and professional failures, I have learned the hard way through many "dark nights of the soul," these powerful key steps for redesigning my life. It is now my honor to pass along these secrets for success.

> *"Without your wounds, where would your power be? The very Angels themselves cannot persuade the wretched and blundering children on earth as can one human being broken in the wheels of living. In love's service, only the wounded soldiers can serve."*
>
> - Thornton Wilder

That is why I wrote this book, to "pass it on." It is my hope you will enjoy assimilating the information and puting its principles into life-enhancing practice. Ultimately, it is my dream that you reap such rewarding success, you will be compelled to "pass it on" and gift those you care about most with their own copy of *The Art of Living*.

> *"The American Dream does not end when it comes true for you. It then becomes your responsibility to help it come true for others."*
>
> - Dr. David Satcher, U.S. Surgeon General

When there is light in the soul,

there is beauty in the person;

When there is beauty in the person,

there is harmony in the home;

When there is harmony in the home,

there is honor in the nation;

When there is honor in the nation,

there is peace in the world.

- Old Chinese Proverb

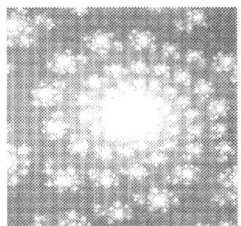